Naked

Beneath

My

Clothes

Naked Beneath My Clothes

TALES OF A REVEALING NATURE

by Rita Rudner

Illustrations by Mike Lester

VIKING

VIKING
Published by the Penguin Group
Viking Penguin, a division of Penguin Books USA Inc.,
375 Hudson Street, New York, New York 10014, U.S.A.
Penguin Books Ltd, 27 Wrights Lane, London W8 5TZ, England
Penguin Books Australia Ltd, Ringwood, Victoria, Australia
Penguin Books Canada Ltd, 10 Alcorn Avenue, Suite 300,
Toronto, Ontario, Canada M4V 3B2
Penguin Books (N.Z.) Ltd, 182–190 Wairau Road,
Auckland 10, New Zealand

Penguin Books Ltd, Registered Offices:
Harmondsworth, Middlesex, England

First published in 1992 by Viking Penguin,
a division of Penguin Books USA Inc.

1 3 5 7 9 10 8 6 4 2

LIBRARY OF CONGRESS CATALOGING IN PUBLICATION DATA
Rudner, Rita.
Naked beneath my clothes : tales of a revealing nature / by Rita
Rudner : illustrations by Mike Lester.
p.   cm.
ISBN 0-670-84462-4
1. American wit and humor.   I. Title.
PN6161.R77   1992
818'.5402—dc20   91-44513

Printed in the United States of America
Set in Gill Sans
Designed by Julie Rauer

This book is dedicated to my parents,
Abe and Frances Rudner,
who always told me I could do anything
but never told me how long it would take.

Acknowledgments

I was going to thank some people but I was afraid I would leave someone out. Then I thought, I'll thank everyone, but I was afraid I would thank some people who didn't deserve to be thanked. So, I decided not to thank anyone because the people who I was going to thank know who they are. Thank you.

Contents

Naked

Beneath

My

Clothes

An Introduction: I Was A Teenage, Pregnant, Alcoholic, Junkie Ninja Hooker

Actually, I wasn't. I just wanted to get your attention. You have just learned the first lesson of show business. Embellish. Make everything about you bigger. (Except your nose. Make that smaller. Immediately.)

After you have made the commitment to embellish, hire a publicity agent to send out a press release that says you despise embellishment of any kind and that you would rather die than be involved in the act of embellishing. Make sure that each press release is accompanied by a photo, and that in the photo you are doing something wacky and wearing something revealing. If interviewed, swear and say something controversial, as this will ensure prominent placement in the newspaper.

If you do not want to do any of these things, I would at this point reconsider professions. If you then still want to go ahead with show business, be prepared to work extremely hard. Along with the frustrations and the anxiety and the bitterness and the humiliation and the degradation, you will have a very good time. And if you are very lucky, someday someone will be interested enough in your points of view to ask you to write a book.

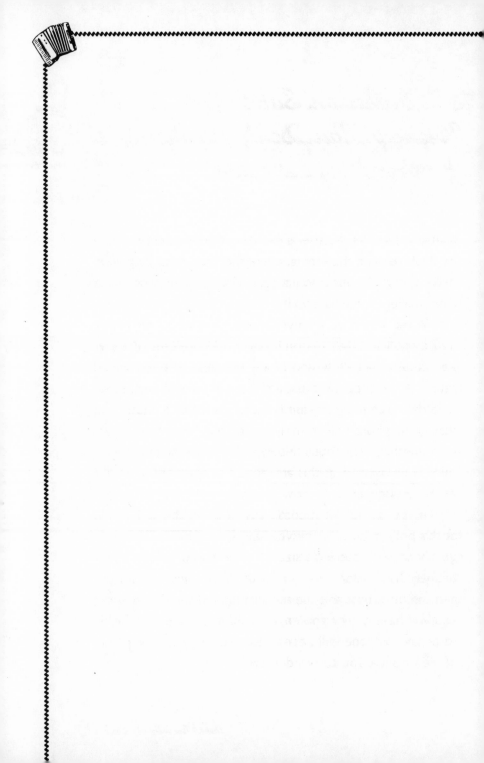

1. It Was on Sale When I Lay Down on It

Buying something on sale is a very special feeling. In fact, the less I pay for something, the more it is worth to me. I have a dress that I paid so little for that I am afraid to wear it. I could spill something on it, and then how would I replace it for that amount of money? Tell me that.

There is another reason I don't wear this dress. I don't like it. I hate the color and I hate the sleeves. But I know that I got this dress (not just a dress, by the way, a *designer* dress) for *less* than *one-third* the original price. God, I'm good.

Another thing about this designer dress . . . it's a *four*. Did you hear me? A *four*. I am usually an eight, but on that day I was thin. That is how designers get you to spend inordinate amounts of money on pieces of material sewn together; the more expensive the garment, the bigger it is cut. Somewhere there is a size six gown that is so expensive it fits Nell Carter.

Stores don't make it easy to buy things on sale. They know women enjoy a challenge. (After all, we marry men.) Certain discount designer dress stores are so intent on making purchasing difficult, they don't even have dressing rooms.

You see those desperate women stuck in various positions of indignity, their arms above their heads and dresses covering their faces, as saleswomen ignore their muffled pleas for help. My favorite thing about these stores is that they are usually located in the middle of nowhere and have nothing but space. What is the addition of a dressing room going to do? Disturb the cow out back?

I do think women actually enjoy this inconvenience, though, and if a dressing room was built, they would ignore it as they would a relative who has been in prison. And you can find very good buys in these stores. I recently bought a beautiful strapless dress that only fits me if I wear it over a pants suit. And it's a very expensive dress, too. Do you want to know how expensive? It's a size two.

All too often I am lured into a store by an "Everything Half Price" sign. After a brief search, I find something that I can't live without, and I take it over to the saleswoman.

"That's not on sale," she tells me, revealing the personality of a dead librarian. She points to a rack of what looks like prison laundry. "Those are on sale."

"What happened to *everything* half price?" I ask.

"*Everything* on that rack is half price," she replies smugly. "You're holding one of our beautiful things that have just come in that you probably can't afford."

I leave, but not empty-handed. The sign is the bait, I am the fish. I have been fileted.

Rita Rudner

The Mona Letterman.

2. How Can I Have Morning Sickness When I Don't Get Up 'Til Noon?

I know lots of women have had children. I've seen them—both the women who have had them and the children they have had. But I'm not sure it's for me. Some women glow, they radiate, they incandess (and that isn't even a word) when they are pregnant.

"Feel the baby kicking, feel the baby kicking," says my friend who is six minutes pregnant and deliriously happy about it. To me, life is tough enough without having someone kick you from the inside.

Upon finding out the test strip turned bluish, yellowish green, my friend (let's call her "Jeremiah," because I don't know anyone called that and I don't want any of my friends to be mad at me) immediately bought one of those books that have pictures of what the baby is doing every day. (I'm not sure it's entirely accurate—in one photo the baby is playing cards.)

"Look at its little veins and fingers and feet," she says.

I feign interest while feeling sick and say, "And I think it has gin."

She looks at me strangely, because I have imagined the photo of the baby playing cards, because I was so bored. Jeremiah kicks me out of her house for not taking the development of her child seriously enough. Jeremiah never could take a joke.

Another friend (for variety's sake I'll call this friend "Phleghh") is a frontier woman. I'm not Danielle Boone. I've never done drugs in my life, but if I ever did have a baby, at that point I would say, "Shoot me up." To me natural childbirth is backward; nowadays everyone takes drugs except when they need them. Phleghh didn't even want to have her baby in a hospital. She preferred a hut. The more mud the better. She didn't want a doctor, either. She wanted a squaw. Phleghh settled on a hospital that was painted taupe and a doctor who liked *Dances with Wolves*. Phleghh was in labor for thirty-six hours. (I don't even want to do anything that feels good for thirty-six hours.) The baby was turned the wrong way. Phleghh had the choice of a cesarean with drugs or writhing in pain in the hope that her unborn child would obtain a sense of direction. Phleghh wanted a cesarean without drugs. I think at this point the unborn child had pity and did an Olga Korbut–like flip. Phleghh is happy and proud that she didn't resort to drugs, but she never did have another baby. Phleggh's baby is now sixteen and does drugs.

It's clear that nature was not altogether fair to women regarding the childbearing process. Other species seem luckier. There's a bird right outside my window that I've been watching as I've been working on this book. She laid some eggs that were an entirely reasonable size, and in a few days they hatched. The results are cute, and now she brings them food. I could deal with that.

Envy the kangaroo. That pouch setup is extraordinary;

the baby crawls out of the womb when it is about two inches long, gets into the pouch, and proceeds to mature. I'd have a baby if it would develop in my handbag. The dolphin just mocks us. I saw a dolphin give birth, and it didn't even stop swimming. It had a baby while working out! Talk about an overachiever.

I know there are all these new and wonderful birthing methods where you put the baby in water or lay it on your stomach and pour warm mushroom-barley soup over it to ease the poor unsuspecting thing into the real world. I'm in favor of a more straightforward approach to life; I think the delivery room should have traffic noise and pollution, and you should immediately put the baby on the phone and have someone be rude to it. The baby should then have the option to go back in.

I guess what I'm trying to say is that some women are cut out for motherhood and some aren't, and I don't know which type I am, but I just reread this chapter and I have a suspicion.

Rita Rudner

I like that pouch setup.

3. I Did, But I Don't Remember When

It's historically one of life's most memorable moments—a man asking a woman to marry him or a woman asking a man. (Women don't really ask. Let's face it, if a relationship gets to this stage, it's more of an ultimatum.) You remember the event in the same way you remember where you were when Kennedy was shot or where you were when you first heard a United States senator saying "Long Dong Silver" on national television.

When a relationship becomes "serious" (I hate that term; it's one step away from "terminal") a woman begins to fantasize about what that very special moment will be like. Will it be in a fancy restaurant? Will I order a shrimp cocktail, and will I spot something shiny in the sauce, and if I don't spot it, does my future husband know the Heimlich maneuver?

Will he hire a plane to write "Will You Marry Me?" in the sky? And if I don't want to marry him, do I then have to hire a plane to write "No"?

What if he's shy and we're on the beach and he writes his proposal in the sand and I'm not paying attention and a big ol' wave comes along and washes it away before I see it? Why didn't he pay more attention to the tide?

Rita Rudner

The other day my friend asked me how my husband proposed. I'm embarrassed to say that my husband and I have been married for over three years now, and I have no idea how it happened. I have a ring. I remember the wedding. The honeymoon is etched on our Visa bill forever, but I can't remember what actually got the ball rolling.

It's not that I have a bad memory. I remember every minute detail of our courtship. I remember where we ate, what I wore, what I spilled on myself, and whether or not it came out, from our first date onward. I can remember things he's mumbled in his sleep from before we were married that I'm waiting for the right time to use against him.

The truth of the matter is, we seem to have skipped over that step in the same way Drew Barrymore skipped over her adolescence. I guess it doesn't really matter; we all got to where we were going. My husband and I are happily married, and Drew is a recovering alcoholic who I'm proud to say has never held up a dry cleaner.

I mentioned this lack of proposal to my husband. He thinks at one point he looked down at his calendar/calculator/microwave watch and said, "We're both in town the weekend of June twenty-fourth."

"And," I said, "what did you say after that?"

"That was it," he said. "We got married June twenty-fourth."

"What about my ring?" I asked.

"I gave you an engagement ring for Christmas the year before," he replied smugly.

"And what did you say when you gave it to me?"

"Here," he said.

"And what did I say when I opened it?"

"I don't know," he said. "You started to cry and sort of make these heaving noises."

Now I remember how all this happened, and as usual, it's all my fault. He asked me what I wanted for Christmas and I said, "A ring." So when he got me a ring and said, "Here," that was it. That was the proposal. That was my special moment. It may not be the proposal most women dream of, but I laughed, I cried, and we've been together for years now. It worked for me, and writing this account has helped me to understand why I get misty-eyed whenever my mailman hands me a package and says, "Here."

4. What Is It with Men and Their Cars?

What is it with men and their cars? I know I've just repeated myself, but it's a question that bears repeating. What is it with men and their cars?

I've never known a man who wasn't deeply attached on a very emotional level to his beloved vehicle. Whether it was a piece of junk or a masterpiece made no difference. They rode in their metal boxes and were in control of their lives. I think I know why so many men are afraid to make a commitment to women. It's because we can't be steered.

My first boyfriend, who shall remain nameless and probably jobless, had an antique car. It was a 1957 Jaguar. Now, 1991 Jaguars are not all that reliable. This car kept falling apart in the garage. Charles Manson had a better chance of getting out than this car did. My boyfriend had bought this car and rebuilt it himself with the care and precision of a surgeon who had very little idea of what he was doing.

I actually went into his apartment one day to find him sitting at his dining room table trying to fix the brakes. I stared at this greasy picture and decided maybe we shouldn't live together or for that matter drive together.

When I suggested he take the car to the shop or, God

forbid, buy a car that worked, he looked at me like I'd just suggested he sleep with his sister. This was his "baby." Someday it would work. He would restore a 1957 Jaguar, and he would drive around the neighborhood for everyone to see. I wished him well. I didn't have that kind of time.

For the sake of my marriage, I'll skip over other boyfriends and their cars and go straight to my husband and his. My husband just bought his "dream car." I won't reveal the manufacturer, but in the early 1940s the makers of this car weren't very nice to Jewish people. My husband says I shouldn't let World War II influence my feelings toward his car. He's always wanted this type of car, and now he has it. He has the car and something more. He has a rattle. This is the most beautiful car you've ever seen, and it comes with its own invisible mariachi band.

No one can find the rattle. The salesman who sold us this car can't hear it. He went deaf about the same time the check cleared. Also the alarm on this car is very temperamental. Often it goes off while we are driving. Concerned citizens write down our license plate number and report my husband and me for stealing our own car.

We hand-wash this car. It can't go through a car wash. It's too delicate. The advertisement on television has a building falling on this vehicle and it coming through intact, but it can't be washed with brushes. It needs a natural sponge and special car shampoo. I think we should put it through a car wash. I think it might fix the rattle.

For all the care my husband takes of his car, he does

exhibit some very strange in-car behavior. Basically, my hus-band has two beliefs in life. He believes in God, and he believes that when the gas gauge is on empty, he still has a quarter of a tank. He thinks the "E" stands for "Eeeggghh, there's still some left." Once we were driving along and we were so low on gas, I didn't know what to do, but I wanted to do something . . . so I turned off the radio.

I don't know why men think their cars don't need gas. I think it's because they love their cars and want to believe their cars love them back. If, in some way, their vehicle will run without the benefit of fuel for a few miles, they will know for sure that theirs is a love that is returned. But a car won't do this for them. To quote a phrase I just made up, "No gasee, no runee."

I'll never understand men and their cars, but I have a little confession to make. There is something comforting about my husband loving cars. When we walk down the street I don't really worry about him looking at other women. More often than not when his head turns he is ogling a Ferrari. If he's going to lust after something, I'd rather it be something that lives in a garage.

Chewing gum after the flavor has gone is like hanging on to a bad relationship.

Rita Rudner

5. Survival of the Fattest

It takes six months to get into shape and two weeks to get out of shape. Once you know this you can stop being angry about other things in life and only be angry about this.

I've belonged to many gyms in my life. I like to take advantage of the special offers. "JOIN NOW!! GET LAST YEAR FREE!!!" "SIGN UP TODAY AND GET A FREE RACQUETBALL MEMBERSHIP FOR ANY FRIEND YOU HAVE WHO'S OVER NINETY!!!!!" "PUT NO MONEY DOWN, YOU WON'T COME ANYWAY!!!!!!!" I love an exclamation point!!!!!!!!!

I think of all the gym ads I've ever seen, my favorite was Cher's. I was checking into a hotel once, and there was a life-size cutout of her, beneath which a caption read:

Cher says, "Excuses won't lift your butt."

Rita says, "There has to be a better way to put that." I'm working on it—so far I only have:

Cher says, "If you're going to dance naked onstage in your forties, you're going to have to spend a lot of time at the gym."

To be fair, Cher is in terrific shape. She may have trouble keeping her relationships together, but, boy, she sure has her butt under control.

I think that's the attraction of fitness. In a world where so little goes right, at least you can repeat a motion umpteen times and see a muscle pop up where flab used to be. The problem is, you have to repeat a motion umpteen times. This is mind-numbingly boring and why you find very few geniuses in a gym.

Aerobics has to be the least appealing activity. I don't even know how this word came into being: "aerobics." I guess gym instructors got together and said, "If we're going to charge ten dollars an hour, we can't call it 'jumping up and down.'"

I took an aerobics class once in Los Angeles. This is the worst of all places to take such a class because everyone in Los Angeles is in great shape. There were pregnant grandmothers in purple leotards who weren't even sweating. Anorexic women balanced bureaus on their shoulders while jumping because the workout just wasn't challenging enough for them. I was exhausted after ten minutes, but, luckily, the class was so crowded, I was wedged between two people who jumped for me and was able to finish the lesson.

I do enjoy yoga. I enjoy any exercise where you get to lie down on the floor and go to sleep. Yoga is basically breathing and stretching yourself into impossible positions. My instructor was very good; he could touch the back of his knees to his teeth . . . while driving. I was never going to be very good at yoga—I can touch the tips of my fingers to my wallet, though, and this is the only movement in America you really need.

I jogged for three miles once. It was the worst three hours of my life. I don't think jogging is healthy, especially morning jogging. If morning joggers knew how tempting they looked to morning motorists, they would stay home and do situps. An old boyfriend of mine still runs the New York marathon every year. I could never figure out what would make ten thousand people run twenty-six miles. Maybe there's a Hare Krishna in back of them going, "Excuse me, can I talk to you for just a second?"

In Los Angeles the "thing" is to have a personal trainer come to your home. This is very expensive, and you yourself still have to do the work while this person to whom you're paying lots of money watches. There is something wrong with this system. I'm waiting until they find a way to hook me up to someone who is doing the exercises and I reap the benefits. That is the only way I'm going to stay fit. Until then, I'll just stay angry.

6. A Moving Experience

Joni Mitchell said, "You don't know what you've got 'til it's gone." I disagree. I think, "You don't know what you've got 'til you've tried to move it."

We had a great house. We didn't really want to move, but we were living within our means and people were starting to talk. We live in Los Angeles, where you are expected to move every two to four years so people can see how well your career is going. Most places people walk into a house and think, This is where I want to live for the rest of my life. In Los Angeles people walk into a house and think, This is where I want to live till my series gets sold into syndication. Los Angeles is a very transient town. It's the only place I know where you can actually rent a dog.

Our house was beautiful, but tiny. "How tiny?" you ask. I did a situp in the living room and broke two lamps. The front door opened onto the backyard. It was a quaint house. It had charm. I wish it had a window. It looked like one of those gingerbread houses you see in candy stores over Christmas, only smaller.

Surely it wouldn't be hard to move. What would it take? Ten, fifteen boxes at the most? Try fifty. Fifty boxes full of things I basically never use, look at, or wear, but that I absolutely can't live without. Of course, our most valuable items don't fit into boxes. Our one original painting and our antique armoire had to ride buckshot. Fortunately I bought lots of that bubble paper. Unfortunately my husband had become addicted to popping the bubbles on the bubble paper and would not rest till every last bubble was popped. He was a man with a mission.

We had hired a moving company that had been rec-ommended to us by someone we barely knew. In Los Angeles that counts as a close personal friend. I was a little suspicious when I heard their name, The Klutzola Brothers, but better the devil who has been recommended. (I called a plumber right from the phone book once, and he tried to fix a leak in my sink through the chimney.)

We packed for three days straight. The more boxes we filled, the more things appeared. It was like a huge bowl of pasta that even though you keep eating it refuses to go down. Friday morning we sat on the stoop and through our bleary eyes watched for the Klutzolas.

Oh, there's something I forgot to mention. This darling little house that we lived in was at the top of a not-so-darling and not-so-little mountain. You got to it up very narrow, winding roads. We should have told them that. They would have brought a smaller truck that they would have been able to turn around. They wouldn't have had to back all of our earthly possessions down the mountain.

The Klutzolas were fast. They beat us to our new house

and broke everything before we even got there. I pointed to the gash in the armoire.

"That was there before, lady, we didn't do it," the head Klutz insisted.

"How did you get it up to the second floor?" I asked. "The stairs looked too narrow."

"We threw it over the balcony," he said proudly.

I didn't want to argue. He was stronger than I. He had just thrown my armoire over the balcony.

We sat among our boxes in our new, improved house, and while I wondered whether we would ever be comfortable in a house that was much more comfortable, my husband popped bubble paper.

We've unpacked now, and I love our new house just as much as I loved our old house. There's only one problem. It's almost time to move. I don't want people to think I'm not doing well.

Rita Rudner

Naked Beneath My Clothes

7. Should I Get My Head Analyzed or Just My Hair?

Nobody is really happy with what's on their head. People with straight hair want curly, people with curly want straight, and bald people want everyone to be blind.

I grew up with very curly hair when it was a fashion to have straight. I tried everything to make my hair look like the girls in the magazines. I woke up with tremendous headaches from sleeping with my hair wrapped around soup cans. (I later learned you were supposed to remove the soup.) I put something that smelled like weed killer on my head and sat under a wind machine, only to emerge with a chest cold and curly hair that smelled like weed killer.

After a few years of very poor results, I decided to give up on the whole head and concentrate on my bangs; if I could just create the illusion of having straight bangs, maybe I could convince everybody that I had made the rest of the hair on my head curly on purpose. I taped my hair to my head religiously every night, and this is very difficult for someone who isn't very religious. During the night my hair would pry itself free from the tape and rebelliously position itself at right angles to my head. The tape, however, remained intact. Every morning I would rip it from my head, exposing raw skin that my curly hair refused to cover. I would then try to cover up the red streaks with makeup. It was not a look that would catch on.

I then gave up on the texture and decided to concentrate on changing the color. Blondes have more fun. They must; how many brunettes do you see walking down the street with blond roots? I didn't intend to "go blond," however; I intended to put something very subtle in my hair called "highlights." I sat in a salon while a man who looked like Rita Hayworth pulled out bits of my hair and wrapped them in tinfoil. He told me he understood what I wanted. The streaks would be so subtle you would hardly even know they were there. Only when the sun hit them would they glow . . . not even glow—glint. My friends would sense I was more beautiful, but they would not be sure why. They would think I'd lost weight. I was moved to one side to sit and process. I looked at magazines, picking out the models that I would be mistaken for once freed from my tin turban. I was transferred back onto my chair, and the foil was removed. I had black hair with white stripes. The Rita Hayworth man thought it looked fabulous. He didn't remember my mentioning "subtle": he thought I wanted "highlights."

"Why pay for something you can't even see?" he said.

Everyone in the salon came over to admire his masterpiece. They tried to convince me that I looked stunning. I tried to convince them that the word they were looking for was "stunned." They were very persuasive, and I walked out of the salon feeling like I had solved my hair. It lightened me and my whole outlook on life. I passed a mother and child on the street. They looked at me. People don't usually look at me. The child spoke.

"Why does that lady have a zebra on her head?" it said.

It's not like I learned my lesson. Next, I tried red. For some reason, when I was twenty-one I wanted to be the same color as an Irish setter. Evidently I wasn't going to be happy 'til I had worked my way through the animal kingdom. I have something important to tell you now. Go get a pencil.

Ready? Underline the next sentence. Red oxidizes. That's what the hairdresser told me. I didn't know what she meant. I said, "So long as it doesn't keep me awake."

My hair started out the color of an Irish setter; in six months it was the color of a baboon's bottom. This is what she meant.

Now that I'm in my thirties things are a little different. Curly hair is no longer frowned upon, but desired. Mine is now on the straight side and I've bought a curling iron. And remember how I wanted lighter hair? It's getting lighter. I'm going gray. I want it dark again. Then I'll be happy.

8. If I Can't Have It All, Can I at Least Have Some of Yours?

It's an age-old problem—can a career woman have children, can a mother have a career? Doesn't that sound like what this chapter should be about? Well, it isn't. It's about something much more important. It's about eating parts of other people's desserts.

I can't remember ever having my own dessert. Even when I was a kid, and birthday cake was being passed around, I remember saying, "No, thank you, none for me. I'll just have a bite of Fred's."

This was obviously news to Fred, but it was very hard for him to say no, as it was my birthday.

I guess it's one of those annoying female things. I've never been out with a man who said, "You have a dessert and I'll just pick at it."

Men either have a dessert or they don't. They make a decision and they live with the consequences. Maybe I haven't read the right articles, but if I'm not mistaken, there aren't very many men who are bulimic.

Not having our own dessert runs in our family. In a restaurant, my father would read the list of desserts aloud: "Chocolate suicide, vanilla hara kiri, coconut Holocaust. Gee, they sound awfully good," he'd tell the waiter, "but no thanks."

My dad would close the menu. My mom would say, "Are you sure? . . . I'll split one with you."

My dad would say, "No, I'm on a diet. Just some coffee."

My mom would turn to me. I was her last chance at something sweet. If I ordered it, anything that happened after that was not her fault. I was a kid, and girl kids are allowed to order desserts until they can spell "cellulite." I would order my favorite dessert: plain vanilla ice cream.

"Good, I'll have a bite of yours, and give her some of that coconut cake with it," my mother would say.

"I hate coconut," I would say. "Don't let it touch my ice cream."

"Bring her the coconut cake on a separate plate," my mother would say. "And put it in the middle of the table with six forks, please. In case anyone at another table wants some, because my daughter doesn't like coconut, my husband is on a diet, and it will be too much for me."

The waiter would return with the ice cream directly on top of the coconut cake, and it would be melting down the sides. I would scream, "Get the ice cream off, get it off, the cake is sickening and it's getting all over my ice cream and I'm going to throw up!"

My mother would gently lift off the ice cream, leaving a healthy bit on the cake, and put it on a separate plate.

"There's still some on it, get it off!" I would scream, being a particularly obnoxious child.

Rita Rudner

"There's none on it now. Aren't you going to have any cake?" she would ask me innocently.

"No, it's disgusting."

She would turn to my father. "Abe?"

"None for me, thanks," he'd say.

"You love coconut cake, it's your favorite. I only ordered it because I thought you would have some."

He'd shake his head. She'd push it over to his side and grab a fork. "Oh, well, I'll put it here in case you change your mind. I'll just have a bite," she'd say in a put-upon manner.

She'd reach across the table, neatly eating it one layer at a time. It guess it was less fattening that way. True to herself and to those around her, she would not finish the cake. She would leave at least one lump of it on the plate. "Does anyone want to finish that?" she'd say. "Rita?"

I'd stick my finger down my throat and mime the act of regurgitation.

"Abe? It's just going to go to waste. Well, I'll just leave it, then." She'd put her fork down.

"Okay, okay," my dad would say, and eat the last piece. He had done it; he had claimed responsibility for the dessert. My mom was happy, and she had achieved her goal—a goal that every woman who is trying to stay thin strives for. She had had her cake, but in her mind she hadn't eaten it.

9. In Sickness and in Sickness

My husband and I have been blessed with good health. This is the type of thing you write just moments before the stroke. Health basically gives you the freedom to agonize about things that have absolutely no importance. Right now I'm furious that UPS did not deliver a coffeepot that I had a hell of a time reordering. I wonder how angry I would be about it if I had a cancerous foot.

The reason I mention cancer of the foot is that that is the latest thing my husband thinks he has. Well, it's not exactly foot cancer, it's more toenail cancer, but it could turn into cancer of the foot at any moment. My husband has also had elbow cancer, cuticle cancer, and even nose hair cancer. He has not let his good health get in the way of his thinking that he could die at any minute.

The other thing my husband has, besides severe hypochondria, is severe mistrust of doctors. Since he is from England, he had to have a blood test in order to get his U.S. visa. The doctor's office we had to go to was not in a great part of town, and to be fair to him, the paint job in the examining room did not inspire confidence. The nurse rolled up his shirtsleeve and tied the rubber hose around his arm.

"This is for gonorrhea and syphilis," she said.

My husband pulled his arm away. "Are you giving it to me?" he shrieked as he ran down the hall. He did not have to be sedated, but he did have to be held down.

We have been together for three years now, and he has had more than a few diseases. The good thing about his diseases is that they seldom last more than a day. The bad thing about them is that they are daily. When we were first married I took these illnesses a lot more seriously than I do now. I remember the first one. We were standing facing each other during the wedding ceremony. The justice of the peace said, "Do you take this woman to be your lawful wedded wife?" My husband said, "Yes." We kissed. My husband began to whisper in my ear. What would his first words as my husband be? "Oh, my darling, I'm so very happy," or, more realistically, "Let's get out of here, I hate all of these people." My husband's first words to me as we were locked in an embrace that symbolized our love were, "Could you take a look at that bump on my neck and see if it's anything?"

This has become my job in our relationship: to look at things on various parts of his body and tell him if they're anything. At this point I have to ask you the same question I have asked him. How would I know? I went to grade school, high school, and ballet school. Where would I have gotten my medical training? Camp? Why does he trust me? I look at a mole that could be something and say with great as-suredness, "It's nothing." What if someday it's something? That is why I bought him the *At Home Medical Book*. Big mistake.

He has read the book from cover to cover. He has been through everything the book has to offer, including labor and menopause. A few months ago my husband got a symptom, the worst symptom you could ever get—he was dizzy. Do you know how many things "dizzy" could be? I do. Every page of our medical book is dog-eared. "Dizzy" could be anything from heart attack to brain tumor to high blood pressure. I was really worried because this symptom was lasting longer than the others. We'd be watching television, he'd look at me and say, "Now. It's happening now. What do you think it is?"

"I don't know," I'd say. "Try changing the channel."

This dizziness continued for several days. Would he go to a doctor? Ha! Armed with his medical book, he set off to our local drugstore to cure himself. He came back with a home diabetes test, a blood pressure–taking kit, a stethoscope, and some paper towels because I'd told him we were out of them. One by one we eliminated the possibilities. He pricked his finger and tested his blood: normal. Blood pressure: normal. Heartbeat: normal. There was only one problem. He was still dizzy.

It was time for me to take charge. I took the book and went back to the drugstore. Using my nonexistent expertise, I cross-referenced each chapter to what was available in the store. I went down each aisle eliminating possibilities. It was then that I spotted it. It was on the shelf right next to the eyedrops. I grabbed the box and somehow knew I had solved the medical mystery. I was Dr. Columbo.

Rita Rudner

I handed the box to my husband. "Eardrops?" he said. "How are these going to help a brain tumor?"

I pointed to the writing on the package: "Dizzy? Try the Ear Wax Home Removal Kit."

"Will it hurt?" he asked. "If it's going to hurt, I'd rather just be dizzy."

"Just try it," I said through gritted teeth. He did, and it worked. My dizzy husband was no longer dizzy; he was just dozy. Now if I could just find something that would cure cancer of the toenail.

Very-small-town video shop.

Rita Rudner

10. The Bikini: What Nazi Thought This Thing Up?

If there ever was a time I looked good in a bikini, I sure don't remember it. No matter what age I was, there was always one area of my body that refused to cooperate. Not that I was ever a bikini sort of a gal. When I was five a relative gave me two polka-dotted slivers of material for my birthday. I held up the top and said, "Thank you very much, Aunt Mabel. This will come in handy if I ever have to blindfold a cat."

I remember my mother wearing sturdy orthopedic bathing suits. They were form-fitting, but they were discreet. They covered a respectable part of her upper leg and had two distinct cups that firmly told her bosoms where they were supposed to be. This is the type of bathing suit I expected to be wearing when I got older—not quite as good as the skirt style from the thirties with leggings underneath, but still acceptable.

What happened? Who decided that ordinary, everyday women when they swim should dress like Las Vegas showgirls? At least showgirls have headdresses to divert your attention and high heels to help the leggy illusion. I guess we could try that, but if there's one thing harder than doing laps in a bikini, it's doing laps in a bikini wearing a headdress and heels.

Of course there are alternatives to the bikini. I wish I could be more excited about them. They still require waxing areas that would be much happier never having met wax. Women really do go beyond the call of duty to attract men. I wonder what a man would do in a similar situation. Let's say someone decided that in order for a man to look attractive in a bathing suit to a woman he had to pour hot wax dangerously near the most sensitive part of his body and have it ripped off at least once every two months. How many men do you think would sign up? I think Evil Knievel would say, "Too risky."

I do hate buying bathing suits. Once I find a bathing suit that doesn't offend the public, I wear it for years. I wear it until the elastic is so fragile that it is see-through and exposes far more of my body than a bikini would. This makes sense when you realize how horrible the experience of trying on a bathing suit is.

Women look forward to shopping for a bathing suit with much the same anticipation that baby seals look forward to clubbing season. Men don't know what we go through, so if you are a man reading this book, I am now going to tell you. (After all, we only wear those skimpy things to look good for you. If it were up to us, we'd wear bathing suits that had feet.) We go into these little cells that have mirrors everywhere, and very cruel lighting, so we can see exactly what's wrong with our bodies from every conceivable angle. I think after you leave those rooms they should offer you some kind of counseling—or at least have a sign on the mirror that says, "Caution: objects in mirror may appear larger."

If there is one specific time during the year that my spirits and coincidentally my bosoms are at their lowest, it is the day the *Sports Illustrated* swimsuit issue comes out. (By the way, wearing swimsuits is a sport like ketchup is a vegetable, but this is a subject for a whole other essay.) The annual tension of who will be on the cover is almost more than I can bear. Will it be Mindy or Corky or maybe Suzette? (These women are so young, they only need one name.) One thing I'm sure of: they will all be sandy and wet and nearly naked, and I will be looking in the Yellow Pages under "Liposuction." I actually did consider liposuction at one point, but then I heard they can accidentally vacuum out internal organs that you're using, so I decided just to forge on with the leg lifts.

I have to be honest and tell you that if leg lifts were going to work on me, they would have done so by now. I've been doing them faithfully for about fifteen years, and the only thing that has gotten thinner is the carpet where I have been doing the leg lifts. But I will not give up. Every year when I see that *Sports Illustrated* issue come out, I know it's time to increase my leg activity. I buy all the women's magazines and read about all the new exercises that are alarmingly similar to all the old exercises. I do my donkey kicks and my pelvic tilts with the hope that this year when

I get in that horrible dressing room I'll look in the mirror and won't see a reflection from the funhouse.

Guess what? This year it wasn't so bad. I found a two-piece bathing suit that isn't cut up to my armpits, has an elastic band that helps hold my stomach in, and has bra cups made out of two army helmets. It took me a long time, but I finally found it: an orthopaedic bikini.

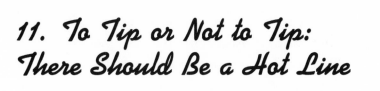

11. To Tip or Not to Tip: There Should Be a Hot Line

My tipping life did not start out well. I was fifteen and had just moved to New York to study dancing. (I know this is shocking to parents of fifteen-year-olds, but this is pretty common among headstrong kids who want to be dancers.) Anyway, I finished my first turkey sandwich in a coffee shop all by myself and picked up my dance bag and strolled out of the restaurant with my feet pointing outward so everyone would know I was a dancer. I didn't get half a block when I heard footsteps running up behind me. I'd only been in New York one day. Was I being mugged already? And aren't they supposed to be quieter than that? The mugger tapped me on the shoulder. I turned around. It was my waiter, and he was angry.

"You forgot to leave me a tip," he said.

"A what?" I said.

"A tip. I served you a turkey sandwich and you gave me nothing."

I panicked and took out my wallet and gave it to him. "Take what you want, just don't hurt me." He took out five dollars and handed me back my wallet.

"That's one dollar for serving you the turkey sandwich and four dollars for making me run down the street."

"Why don't you take two dollars for serving me the sandwich and three dollars for running down the street," I said, still not fully understanding the concept.

He looked at me the same way I have seen many people look at me through the years and said, "Okay."

As he strutted away I suddenly realized why, when we ate out in restaurants, my parents always left money on the table. Up until then I just thought they were forgetful. My parents told me about lots of things in preparation for my moving to New York—murderers, muggers, rapists, and even which relatives to avoid—but they forgot to tell me whom to tip.

I'm totally confused in hair salons, so I stay out of them. I went to an exclusive hair salon in New York City once, and I swear Jacqueline Onassis was in front of me asking the lady behind the counter, "Whom do I owe money to, and how much?" I figured she had been frequenting hair salons for quite a few years and if she still didn't know, there was no hope for me. I've simplified that part of my life. I now have a very nice man who comes to my house and cuts my hair in the backyard, and he tells me how much I owe him and I pay and he seems happy.

Don't get me wrong; I don't mind tipping. I'm glad to have the money to tip with. I just wanted to do it well. I do think that there is something fundamentally wrong with the system. If tipping is supposed to make people do a better job, I think it should be upfront, and I think two other professions should be added to the tip list: pilots and surgeons. These are people to whom you should definitely slip an extra ten.

The other tipping festival I have encountered is in five-star hotels. I recently arrived in New York City, and after tipping the taxi driver for almost killing me at an intersection and for making me listen to Arabic music for two hours, we pulled up to a fancy hotel. A guy wearing an outfit that I hoped he hadn't had to buy took my suitcase out of the cab. Another guy took my suitcase to the check-in desk. Yet another guy took it up to the room. I just tipped anyone who touched it. A guy tripped over it, I gave him a dollar and a half.

I know about waiters now, and I know how much. I just double the first number of the total and add another couple of dollars on top of that if they recognize me. There is now, however, something else I don't understand. When I pay for my meal with a credit card there are four spaces —total, tip, captain, and "other." I have the first two categories under control, but who is the captain and, more important, who is "other"? Am I supposed to look around and leave money to patrons who clean their plates? I just cross these sections out and leave very fast, so if either "captain" or "other" comes running up behind me on the street, I'll at least have a head start.

Naked Beneath My Clothes

12. It's a Boy, It Weighs Twenty-four Pounds, and It's Got Giblets

I loved my mother very much, but she was not a good cook. Most turkeys taste better the day after; my mother's tasted better the day before. In our house Thanksgiving was a time for sorrow. Consequently, for years my recipe for a Thanksgiving turkey was to take one cab to my friend Julie's house.

Thanksgiving at Julie's house was always a community effort. Everybody who came had to bring something to dinner. I was usually assigned something that could not be ruined . . . like the forks. For some reason, when it comes to cooking, I don't inspire great confidence in people. I wasn't happy with my fork assignment, however, and I was determined to work my way up the ladder of Thanksgiving trust. I graduated from silverware to salad, and then one particular year the guy who usually brought the pies, John, was in a play and wasn't able to attend.

I was very excited about being assigned the pies. The pies are a very important part of the Thanksgiving experience, even though by the time pie time comes, no one has any room for them. I called Julie up the day before to confirm my assignment.

"Hello, Julie, this is Rita, the pie woman. I'll be there

at three-thirty. I'm just checking on what kind of pies and how many I should bring," I said.

"Just make four," she said. "Two pumpkins, an apple, and a mincemeat will be more than enough."

I hung up the phone. I called her back. "Did you say 'make'? Why did you say 'make'?"

"Everyone makes the things they bring, that's part of the fun," she insisted.

I hung up the phone again. I called her back again. "Do you think you could get in touch with John? It's going to be much easier for me to replace him in the play than it's going to be for me to make these pies."

Julie told me not to panic and that anyway I was wrong for the male lead in *Man of La Mancha*.

I made the pies, but I didn't make the crusts, although I said I did. They were pretty good, if I do say so myself, but I bought four backup pies from the bakery in case mine really stank. I clearly "overpied" and the next year was just asked to bring a bag of marshmallows and stay out of the kitchen. I didn't argue.

It was just last year that I got up enough cooking confidence to tackle a turkey. My husband, being English, did not really know what a Thanksgiving turkey should taste like, so I figured no matter what happened I could just say, "This is how it's supposed to be; the Pilgrims liked it chewy."

I went to the grocery store the day before the event. I walked up to the poultry person and said proudly, "Give me your smallest turkey." The man, in a gesture that could

Naked Beneath My Clothes

only be described as a hoist, hoisted up the biggest turkey I'd ever seen. This was no ordinary turkey; this was a Schwarzenegger turkey.

"You don't understand," I said. "It's just for two people. This will feed several states."

"This is the smallest I have left, lady. If you wanted a smaller bird, you should have ordered it."

I hate learning through experience. Just once I'd like to learn something because someone was nice enough to tell me it in advance. I brought Schwarzenegger home and consulted my turkey book. Did you know that cooking a turkey involves sewing? I didn't. I went back out and bought my turkey trussing set. I washed it, I stuffed it, I buttered it, I dropped it. I picked it up and started over again.

I basted for hours, and in between basting sessions I made potatoes, brussels sprouts, and salad. The turkey was ready. I called my husband; it was going to take two of us to move this sucker. We got it to the table. We rested. My husband carved (this is the man's contribution to the Thanksgiving process), and as we sat down to eat my husband turned to me and asked, "Where's the gravy?"

"The Pilgrims didn't like gravy," I told him, and quickly changed the subject. Gravy had never occurred to me. I kind of figured the turkey made its own gravy. Do I have to do everything?

The turkey was tasty, which was a good thing because we had it for weeks. We had turkey leftovers, turkey sandwiches, turkey soup. I got so attached to the turkey, at the end I put the bones back together and had a little puppet show.

Next year I think I'm going to be brave enough to invite people over to my house for Thanksgiving, but I'm going back to the community effort system. Everyone who comes has to bring something. I've already invited Julie; she's bringing the turkey.

13. Things You'll Never Hear Me Say in a Restaurant

1. I make this much better.
2. Waiter, I'm afraid you left that glass of wine I had off the bill.
3. Yes, I'll have a dessert.
4. Could you please take this back to the kitchen, it's lousy.
5. My mother makes this much better.

The Intensive Hair Unit.

Naked Beneath My Clothes

14. A Patient Man (and Other Things That Don't Exist)

"P.C.O.," my father would yell from the kitchen. "Did you hear me, Frances? P.C.O."

My mother would scream from the bedroom, "I'm coming, I'm coming!"

P.C.O. was the abbreviation for "Pulling the Car Out." Once my father did that, my mother would have approximately one more minute to get herself ready. If there was anything unfinished at that point, it would have to be done in the car. You know those little mirrors that are on the back of sun visors over the passenger's seat of most cars? I'm sure they were invented by the wife of an impatient car designer. My mother was a highly skilled woman. Not many people can curl their eyelashes, comb out their hair, and eat a bowl of hot cereal in a vehicle traveling forty-five miles an hour.

I never really understood why my father was in such a hurry all the time, especially in the morning. What would have been the big deal if he was a few minutes late to his job? My father was self-employed. What was he going to do—fire himself? My mother was his secretary. He certainly couldn't fire her; it would leave her free to shop.

When I was growing up I thought this pathologically impatient behavior was peculiar to my father. I didn't know it was going to apply to every man I've ever met. I recently read that boys are born prematurely much more often than girls. Evidently their impatience starts in the womb.

My first boyfriend never even came into the house to announce his arrival. He'd just sit in his car in our driveway and honk. "Hurry up," my father would say. "Don't keep him waiting."

"Why are you concerned about him? I thought you said you hated him," I'd say.

"I do hate him," he'd reply. "I just don't want him to have to wait."

There is a big difference in what goes on before men and women leave the house. Men get dressed, women get ready. My husband brushes his teeth, puts on his clothes, and he's ready to face the world. I brush my teeth, put on my clothes, and I'm ready to face the mirror. I never wear makeup when I'm at home, and I'm not sure why. For some reason, in front of the man I want to attract I can look terrible; in front of people I'm never going to see again, I have to look my best.

My husband does a sneaky thing to me; he changes the rules in the middle of the game. He looks at his watch and announces, "All right, it's six o'clock. We leave at six-thirty."

"Six forty-five," I plead. "We aren't due at the restaurant 'til seven-thirty, and it's around the corner."

"There will be traffic," he argues.

"There is always traffic. That is why they built roads . . . for traffic," I argue back.

He looks at his watch again. "We'll compromise. Six thirty-six. You have twenty-seven minutes and thirteen seconds. . . . *Go.*"

He fires an imaginary gun in the air. I time everything perfectly—ten minutes for hair, ten minutes for makeup. I am just about to use my last seven precious minutes for choosing my clothes when I hear him downstairs.

"You ready yet? It's six-thirty," he yells.

"What happened to six thirty-six?" I yell nakedly.

"I said six thirty-six at the outside. Six-thirty was the time we originally discussed."

And then I hear it. "I'll be waiting for you in the car," he says.

My father is a Jewish lawyer born in upstate New York, my husband is a Protestant theatrical producer who was born in London, and they have come up with the same solution: to sit in the car. They have absolutely nothing in common, and they are the same person.

There is one big difference: while my father demanded my mother's presence in the car immediately, my husband in his approach adds the word *wait*. It's not much, but it's B.T.N. (better than nothing).

Rita Rudner

15. Undeveloped Talent

A few years ago, someone bought me an expensive camera. It had this lens that you had to focus and it needed some special film and a green light came on if the subject was too close and a red light came on if the subject was Presbyterian. There was no way I could ever figure out this camera. I just bought a black outfit and wore it as a necklace.

The flash cube is something that has let me down more consistently than my first boyfriend. This is how it usually goes—I get the people who I want to immortalize in a group, I raise the camera, I aim, I apologize.

Cameras are very easy to use now. The last camera I bought guaranteed great shots, no risk involved. It came with pictures of people I didn't know.

Once, when I was young and single (I was old and single, too, but at the time of this particular story, I was young and single) I went on a vacation to Paris with a friend. My friend made me buy a camera for the trip and called me six times before our flight to remind me to bring it. There are many beautiful things in Paris, and I took lovely pictures of them from our tour bus window. Unfortunately, most of the pictures had a tour bus window curtain obscuring all but a small portion of the beautiful things.

My friend couldn't believe how bad my pictures were when I showed them to her. Fuzzy, crooked, double-exposed. It was like seeing Paris through the eyes of a drunk. I was very depressed when I saw them, too. I thought I'd had a much better time.

Camera incompetence runs in our family. My father has seen many cameras in his lifetime. Whenever he is handed one he looks at it, goes into a rabid, foaming fit, and bellows, "What do I do, where do I look, what do I push?" I explain everything to the best of my ability, and he takes two photos: one of his finger and one of his stomach.

My mother was a little better. She could take pictures; what she couldn't do was stick them in a book. She could stick them in a bag, where they could stick to each other. If anyone ever wants to see my baby pictures, they'll have to settle for just seeing the top one.

I did remember to bring a camera to my wedding. Because we were married in a courthouse it wasn't a very formal affair. I had one picture left on the roll. I found a stranger in the courthouse hall minutes after we were married and asked her to take our picture. Unbeknownst to me, behind us was a soda machine and a very thirsty man. Our official wedding picture has three people in it: two of them are smiling and one of them is drinking a Diet Coke.

My husband brought his camera on our honeymoon. He had a roll of film in it that he'd been trying to finish for eleven years. He took pictures of me on our balcony over-looking the sea, in the pool, we even set the timer and unintentionally took pictures of furniture. We couldn't wait to get them back.

"How old was the roll of film in this camera?" I asked when we picked the photos up.

"Why?" he replied. "Didn't they come out?"

They came out all right. There were pictures of me, and there were also pictures of women I didn't know. This rare piece of film enabled me to see my husband's girlfriends throughout the ages. You know how, if you flick through pictures real fast, you can see the image move? Well, if I flick through these pictures real fast, I don't get as angry.

Somewhere in our house we have three cameras. My husband and I each brought one camera to our marriage, and I bought another one just last year. I don't know where any of these cameras are, but I hope they're happy. I have had my picture-taking privileges taken away and no longer need them.

My friends Ian and half of Julie before we left for Paris.

Rita Rudner

Trees in front of the Notre Dame.

Naked Beneath My Clothes

The Eiffel Eiffel Tower Tower.

Rita Rudner

A building that moved just as I
took its picture (Paris).

The curtain on the bus partially
obscured by the Arc de Triomphe.

Rita Rudner

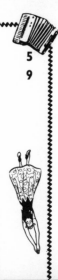

Acrobats (look closely).

Naked Beneath My Clothes

16. Flirting with Success

Flirting is genetic; some women just have that look in their eye that says, "I'm a friendly, happy person who you might have a good time with." I happen to have a look in my eye that says, "You come near me and I'll call the police."

I started this distancing behavior when I was very young. Most kids can't wait to get past the red velvet rope to sit on Santa's lap. I stood on the outside of the ropes and shouted, "Get a pencil. I'll tell you what I want from here." I guess some of it also has to do with your parents. My father was never very friendly. When I was growing up, I thought the doorbell ringing was a signal to pretend you weren't home.

Being a comedian means that I've spent literally thousands of nights in night clubs waiting to do my act. When people ask me how I dealt with men hitting on me night after night, I have to make things up. I tell them, "There were many times when I had to resort to defending myself using my skills from the Far East."

"Karate?" they ask.

"No, chopsticks," I reply. (I'm allowed. I'm a comedian.)

The truth is, no one really bothered me. I'd sit in the

corner of the club with my notebook and work on new jokes. If an unwanted suitor ever approached, I did have a technique for getting rid of him. If a stranger walked up and said, "So, what do you do?" I'd reply in broken English, "I'm no speaking your language very well. I in country to try to get my brother out of prison. You help?" That's usually enough to send men running.

I've never really understood some of the standard flirting methods. Why are women wearing perfumes that smell like flowers to attract men? Men don't like flowers. I have a great idea for a scent that will attract men—how about "New Car Interior"? And what are men wearing? Why do they think women like horse saddles and pine sap? If a man wanted me to follow him down the street, he should wear something called "Butter Cookie" or, even better, "Croissant."

Blondes are generally better at flirting than brunettes. My best friend in junior high and high school was and is a blonde. She was captain of the cheerleaders. She was always showing off how limber she was. In our yearbook, in her head shot, she has her leg in it. She always had a look about her that made people want to seek her out and say, "Where's the party?" I had a look that made people want to seek me out and say, "What's the matter?"

Our facial expressions aside, we've remained best friends through the years, and she's even tried to coach me into being more aggressive when I saw someone I might like. I met one man I thought I might like while doing a show in New York. I told her about him and that I would probably never see him again and that I was much too shy to call him. She encouraged me to find out his address and write him a note inviting him over to my house for dinner. I did. He came, he brought a date, and he was homosexual. Other than that, the evening turned out perfectly.

I didn't attempt flirting again for a few years, but before I did I made sure to get some back story. This next victim of my femininity turned out to be my husband. He's a theatrical producer, and I met him when he hired me to do a show. I worked for him for two years before we got together. To give you an idea what a slow worker I was, I slept with the producer after I already had the job, which in Hollywood is pretty unusual. We recount our getting together slightly differently. We were out to dinner with a group of people, and I maintain that I made it clear that I was attracted to him by brushing up to him suggestively in a restaurant. He claims that I tripped and fell into him on the way to our table, I didn't talk to him for the rest of the evening and after dinner he walked me to my room so he could ask me, "What's the matter?"

Either way, it happened. I no longer have to worry about who's going to give what signal to whom and what it is going to mean and is the person I'm sending the signal to who I think they are. The pressure is off, and I'm finding it much easier to flirt.

Rita Rudner

An early attempt by Rita at flirting.

17. Acting in the Movies

A long time ago, while my father was watching *The Graduate* in a movie theater, someone stole his car. This ruined going to the movies for him. My father hasn't been inside a movie theater since 1976 . . . and he still hates Dustin Hoffman. My husband's father claims he caught pneumonia in a movie theater around that same time and also considers watching movies at home less of a risk.

These are nothing but convenient excuses. It's not that I think these things didn't happen. I know for a fact they did. But there is a point in life when it's easier to be in an environment you can control, where people will be quiet and where your feet won't stick to the floor. That point in my own life is not that far off.

I'll go to the movies, but it has to be a movie I really want to see. The official movie ratings are "General," "Parental Guidance," and "Restricted." I have my own ratings. They are "See at Movie Theater," "Wait for Video," and "Not Even If/When It Comes on Cable Someone Comes to My House and Staples My Eyes Open."

Recently my husband and I went to see "a summer blockbuster." The theater was packed, and there were two teenage girls sitting behind us catching up on old times. I turned around and, doing my best impression of an adult, said, "Why do you come to the movies?"

They looked at me and replied, "To talk."

"Fair enough," I said. "You wait here. I'll get someone to turn down the movie."

They said, "That's all right, we can hear each other."

I turned to my husband, who refused to get involved, and said, "I've taken care of the situation. The girls can hear each other."

"Shhhh," the people next to me said. "Were you raised in a barn? We're trying to hear the movie."

The girls behind me continued talking, and for some strange reason, they didn't bother the people sitting next to me. I gave up.

I'll never understand why people go to movie theaters to have conversations. Going to the movies to talk is like going to a restaurant to cook. The idea is that you have paid your money to have someone do something better than you can do it yourself. You don't go to a racetrack to take a turn at the wheel. (This reminds me, and this is important, if you haven't already seen it, don't see *Days of Thunder*. Don't ask me why, just trust me.)

There is appropriate talking in movie theaters. "What did he say?" "Why did he do that?" "Where are they going?" These are all acceptable phrases in a modulated tone of voice because there are many movies that are impossible to figure out. These movies usually star Mickey Rourke. Boy, can he mumble. I never know what he is saying. Maybe that's why he's so popular in France; maybe he's speaking French. Mickey Rourke is the mumble king of the mumble movies. (Why is it that the mumble movies are usually the movies that have the complicated plots? In the movies that have no plots everyone has perfect diction.)

Another thing that makes movies very difficult for me to watch in movie theaters is popcorn. It's such a loud food, and people get so carried away. Of course the appeal of popcorn for theater owners is its mark-up value. Four dollars a bucket. Popcorn costs . . . what? thirteen cents a silo? I urge theater owners to rethink movie food and mark up something quieter. Maybe bags of sliced tomatoes.

Lately, lots of people have been bringing their babies to the movies, and their babies aren't happy about it. I wouldn't be happy either if I were two months old and someone brought me to see *Drugstore Cowboy*. I don't think that the parents of these babies are bringing these babies to the movies. I think the parents of the babies go out to dinner and the baby-sitter brings the baby to the movies. The only good thing I can say about babies crying in the movies is that it drowns out the noise of the people eating popcorn.

Because my husband and I are in show business and don't work during the day, we've started going to the movies in the afternoon. There are two other types of people who go to the movies in the afternoon: people who have retired and people who have escaped. Both these types of people make strange noises, and you don't want to mess with them.

The times have changed. When I was a kid, smoking marijuana in a movie theater was pretty common. The latest thing that has happened in Los Angeles movie theaters is shootings that are not on the screen. I know directors strive for realism, but when I go to see *Fantasia*, I don't expect my handbag to turn into a clarinet. Similarly, when I go see an action movie, I don't require a flesh wound.

So I've started watching more movies at home. It's safer and the popcorn is cheaper, but I still can't figure out what Mickey Rourke is saying.

The Indians saw the Big Dipper, the Little Dipper, the Milky Way.
Beverly saw necklaces.

Rita Rudner

18. Getting Cold Feet

My husband is usually hot, I am usually cold, and my feet are usually freezing. This is the nightly weather report from our bedroom. If I raise the temperature in the room high enough to warm my feet, I will cook my husband.

My husband initially didn't want me to wear socks to bed. Then, very early in our relationship, during what can only be described as a crucial moment (we were watching the end of a Hitchcock film we hadn't seen), he felt my feet up against his. He let out a scream, and we still don't know why the man in the movie killed his wife; my husband insists it must have had something to do with her feet. He now encourages the use of foot covers, and although naked with socks isn't a look that is featured in the Victoria's Secret catalog, it works for us.

I don't know why my feet get so cold at night. They aren't cold during the day—in fact, they tend to get a little sweaty. When I'm sitting around in the evening watching TV, they're such a comfortable temperature I wouldn't even know I had feet. However. I get into bed . . . feetsicles.

I've tried different foot-warming techniques through the years. One pair of socks is not enough. My feet are still cold, and I run the risk of them coming off during the night and frostbite setting in. I wrapped my feet in Saran Wrap for a while, and though they stayed warm, they got thinner, which caused my shoes to flap. The multisock method works the best for me. I put two socks on each foot (usually a poly-cotton blend underneath and a wool on top to avoid irritation). I fall asleep, and my feet gradually begin to heat up. About one forty-five in the morning I carefully peel off one sock from each foot. I do this carefully not out of respect for the socks, but so as not to wake my husband.

"What are you doing?" my husband asks.

"Nothing," I lie.

"You're not taking your socks off, are you?"

"Maybe." I test the waters.

"Why are you taking them off?"

"My feet are too hot." I come clean.

"I hate your feet." He comes cleaner.

"I'm aware of that, but when you married me you didn't just marry me up to the ankles. My socks are off now. Go to sleep."

He turns over and mumbles something about next time around marrying someone with circulation. He goes back to sleep, unaware that I still have one pair of socks to go. I fall asleep; my feet again begin to heat up. About four thirty-six I am again feeling the need to desock. I peel them more carefully, if that is possible, but this time I only take them half-off, just in case my feet get cold again and I want to be able to put them back on with a minimum of fuss. After all,

Rita Rudner

I wouldn't want to go searching around in the bed and run the risk of waking my husband.

"What are you doing now?" he asks.

"Maybe," I say, cutting to the chase.

"It has something to do with socks, doesn't it? Are you putting them back on?"

"You don't really want to know," I intuit. "Just go back to sleep."

He does. I follow. As I suspect, my feet begin to get cold. The pair of socks I balanced so beautifully on my toes have felt the need to be free. At this point I can either go on a very subtle hunt in the bed or tiptoe to my sock drawer. I tiptoe so quietly, I leave out the tip. I open my sock drawer. It is empty. It seems that all of my socks are currently in the bed. Left with only the subtle-hunt-in-the-bed alternative, I look up. My husband is holding what can only be described as a shitload of socks.

He says, "I married a centipede. Do you want any of these?"

"Yes, thank you."

I take the socks and put them in the drawer. No need for them now. It is almost dawn and my feet are already beginning to get a little sweaty.

19. Comfortable with Age

Question: What do the pope and Hugh Hefner have in common?

Answer: They both go to work in their robes.

Although I don't admire Hugh Hefner and do admire the pope (I have a lot of respect for anyone who can tour without an album), I do think they both have the right attitude toward clothing. The looser the better. My motto is, "If it fits, don't wear it."

I'm lying a little—on television and onstage I have to wear nice things or else people will begin to feel sorry for me, but offstage sweat pants prevail ninety percent of the time. Jogging outfits are desirable for many reasons. When you wear them while out doing errands, people cannot be sure whether you're wearing them because you've just exercised or are about to exercise. Either way, you make them feel guilty. (If you really want to spoil their day, add a headband.) An added bonus about these clothes, of course, is that if you actually do decide to exercise, there is no messy changing.

The other group of people who I really feel understand

Rita Rudner

dressing for comfort is nuns. I love the head thing that enables them to only worry about an inch of hair in the front; I love the long black dresses with the loose-fitting belts that disguise any weight problem; but most of all, I love the shoes. Nothing looks more comfortable to me than a good, solid pair of nun's shoes.

A study was recently done on high heels. The government spent over five million dollars to conclude that women shouldn't stuff their feet into pointy-toed boxes offset at the other end by spikes. They could have saved their money and just taken a look at my aunt Sylvia's feet. Her toes form a little layer cake right in the middle of her foot. I remember when I was little I used to love to go into my aunt Sylvia's closet and try on her high heels. I couldn't wait until I grew up and all of my toes would be in the middle. They were swerving in that direction when it became acceptable to wear sneakers. The problem with sneakers is that they are a day shoe. When I get dressed up for a wedding or a circumcision or something, they are noticeably not right. What I like about nun's shoes is that they're always appropriate. You can wear them any time of day and they can go anywhere, although for the life of me I don't know what a nun would be doing at a circumcision.

When I was a teenager I used to have a pair of very tight jeans. These jeans were so tight that when I zipped them up my nose got bigger. I couldn't wear these jeans for long periods of time without getting very cranky, but for the few minutes a day I could jam myself into them I felt

Naked Beneath My Clothes

svelte. It got to the point where I could only tolerate these jeans for a few seconds a month. I'd struggle for hours, and when I'd got them zipped up I'd throw my hands over my head like a gymnast who had completed a successful vault and try to get the hell out of them. It meant a lot to me to be able to fit into these jeans. I suffered a broken thumb and dislocated spleen, and I didn't even win a medal for my country. Eventually, I remember one day looking down at the two sides of the zipper separated by my stomach and thinking that it would be easier to unite the Middle East. The jeans were put to rest, and I wrote a letter to Golda Meir.

When I do have to look good, and I know comfort is not an option, my compromise to myself now is to buy a dress that works for me. It has to either push something out, hold something in, or cover something up. You have to look long and hard for these dresses, because most designers are male and most of them, how can I put this, are not overly familiar with women's bodies. I certainly don't care about anyone's sexual preference, but I do feel that these designers should do a little homework and at least ask their mothers to fill out questionnaires. A few helpful hints regarding hips and bosoms and they would stop making dresses that only look good on a street lamp.

Popelike, my husband practically lives in his robe. I've asked for a nun's outfit for Hanukkah. We may not be in fashion, but we're comfortable, and if we ever feel like praying, we're ready.

Rita Rudner

The work of Marcia Fitz—makeover artist-underachiever.

20. Inhuman Nature

~~I'm a pretty nice person. I'm not a bad person. I'm no Mother Teresa. I'm somewhere between Mother Teresa and Hitler.~~ I try to be the best person I can be, but I'm constantly letting myself down. Human nature is largely something that has to be overcome. Lots of the little things in life that give me pleasure are usually connected with someone else's misfortune. Not big misfortunes, not even misfortunes, more inconveniences; little victories in my life that keep me going. Before you start to hate me, let me give you a few examples and see if they sound familiar.

1. You're standing on line for a very popular movie. You're worried about whether or not you will get in. You wait ten minutes. You turn around. You are no longer at the end of the line. There are now at least thirty people behind you who have less chance of getting in than you do, and if they do, you will almost certainly get a better seat. What is your reaction? Do you say to the people behind you, "Hey, you can all get in front of me, I can see this movie tomorrow night." No, you gloat—admit it, you gloat . . . or am I the only one?

Rita Rudner

2. I'm staying in a hotel, and while walking down the corridor I always peek in other people's hotel rooms to see if they are nicer than mine. If their room is nicer, I rationalize to myself, "It's just a room, I'm going to be sleeping in it most of the time." However, if my room is nicer, I think, "Ha ha, I got a better room, ha, ha, ha, ha, ha, ha, ha, ha." I revert to a three-year-old and say "ha" far too many times.

3. We all know that life isn't fair; but restaurant service should be. When I sit down at a restaurant and the people who sit down fifteen minutes after me get served first, I'm furious, unless I'm the later person who has gotten served. I don't wait and say, "I'm not eating until the people who got here before me are taken care of." I eat. I eat, and it's especially delicious.

4. There are few things that have given me more joy than Geraldo Rivera being hit in the nose by a chair. It still gives me the giggles when I think about the bandage. I don't like Geraldo Rivera, but I would never wish him harm. I just think it's the chair that makes the image special. A fist would have been too common and a blender too disturbing, but a chair and a nose coming together when the nose belonged to Geraldo Rivera, that was a delight.

5. This is something that must not go farther than this book. Sometimes, when I'm in an elevator and I see someone running toward it, I . . . I . . . I pretend I can't find the Open Door button. There, I said it. It has nothing to do with the character of the person who wants to come in. I don't even particularly want to be alone. I just don't want to press the button.

6. When I'm driving down the street and see someone else fixing a flat tire, I sit a little taller. I know someday that will be me out there, but it hasn't happened yet, so I'm still able to chuckle.

7. In traffic there is only one rule that is a constant. The lane of traffic that you are in is the lane of traffic that isn't moving. If I were in the lane of traffic that was moving, I'm sure I would be happy about it, but this personally has never happened to me.

8. I'm in the movie theater, a woman with an enormous head sits down directly in front of the person sitting next to me. I am amused, but only for a few seconds before she changes her mind and sits directly in front of me.

9. One of my very best friends who has never been able to gain weight (poor thing) recently gained ten pounds and had to go on a diet. Glee. I call her and laugh and hang up. (She does deserve it; all those years of complaining to me about the horrors of having to drink a chocolate shake every day.)

Rita Rudner

10. My husband found a gray hair on his head. He was upset. I had it framed.

There are more things about myself that I'm ashamed of, but I'm going to stop here, just in case it's not really human nature . . . and I'm the only one.

21. Public Speaking

"Ever since my mother died of breast cancer, I've been unable to relate to my boyfriend sexually."

"How long has it been since you've slept together?"

"Over six months. I've begged him to come to therapy with me, but he feels if I'm frigid, it's my problem."

This is the conversation that I tried not to overhear from the women sitting in the far corner of a restaurant. Why, I wonder, do some people want to say the most personal things at rock concert volume? Do they want the other people in the restaurant to join in?

My back was turned, I was seated across the room, and I was trying to eat an omelet. I reasoned, before I judged these people too swiftly and too harshly, that there are excuses. Maybe they were both hard of hearing and because of a skiing accident all of their arms were broken and they couldn't use sign language. Maybe woman number one's boyfriend was a waiter in the restaurant and she wanted to embarrass him. Maybe they were really young and hadn't been out in public much and did not know how to behave. I would have accepted any of the above.

Rita Rudner

I slowly turned around. They were both healthy-eared, able-armed women in their forties. I, a total stranger, knew about woman one's mother, boyfriend, and libido in great detail. I can only assume that she wanted it that way.

To be fair, I'm a little overly sensitive to people speaking loudly because my parents never spoke loudly, even in our house. Come to think of it, I can't remember anyone ever speaking at all. I practically had to lip-read the TV, and my father watched football with the sound off because he lived in fear of hearing the voice of Howard Cosell.

I've always thought that conversations in public should be strictly between the people involved. I could never understand why people talked so freely in taxis. When I was a kid I thought that one of the requirements for being a taxi driver was that you had to be deaf. I never quite figured out how the driver could hear your destination, but then I was a kid.

Conversations in public have reached new decibels with the advent of the portable phone. Recently my husband and I were having lunch with my in-laws while a woman at the next table dialed everyone she ever knew and screamed her thoughts through bad connections. My mother-in-law, who, trust me, you don't mess with, inquired as to whether the woman might be eating or leaving any time soon. The woman explained that her phone at home was broken and these calls were all absolute emergencies. Her next call was a classic; she picked up the phone, she dialed, she screamed through the static, "Hello, Mary, this is Ginger, what's new?"

Naked Beneath My Clothes

We left the restaurant, and my mother-in-law gave Ginger our bill.

Everyone talks about the dangers of drinking and driving, but the dangers of drinking and talking are quite severe, too. You have no idea what you're saying, and everyone can hear you. There are only two times those factors come together: you're either drunk or you're president.

Americans do talk more loudly than the people in other English-speaking countries. The first time I went to England I had to rely on my years of lip-reading the television until my ear adjusted. I was having dinner alone one night in a restaurant in London, and the couple right next to me was having an argument. I couldn't hear a thing; I could just tell by the hand movements and facial expressions that they weren't getting along. Feeling a little homesick, I leaned over and said, "Excuse me, I'm from America. Could you please speak up?"

Rita Rudner

Bob and Mavis bitterly regretted hiring the Hare Krishna Gardening Company.

Naked Beneath My Clothes

22. Thirty-Five and Holding

At the end of every year, I add up the time that I have spent on the phone on hold and subtract it from my age. I don't count that time as really living. I spend more and more time on hold each year. By the time I die, I'm going to be quite young.

Sometimes I spend what seems like hours on hold only to be mysteriously disconnected before speaking to anyone. These times are so disturbing to me that I feel I am justified in subtracting not only from my age but also from my weight.

I also enjoy the little warnings you get when on hold, like "Do not hang up; your call is being ignored in the order received." I have a hold limit that I've set for myself. I hold until I start to imagine myself killing the person on the other end. Then I hang up and regroup.

Lots of companies play music on the phone. Why? What are you supposed to do? Dance? If their intentions are legitimate and they want to entertain you, they could at least ask you what you want to hear. Instead I'm usually forced to listen to one of my favorite songs massacred by an orchestra on Valium. "Born to Run" was not written for the violin.

Rita Rudner

What sadist invented "call waiting"? Now I'm not just talking on the phone with my friend, I've inadvertently entered a popularity contest. Who is more important to my friend—me or the mystery caller on line two? I have to admit call waiting does open up new phone possibilities. I was speaking with someone the other day who put me on hold, and while I was on hold I got a call and put them on hold. When the original caller came back to me, he informed me that he had someone currently on hold. We had achieved a triple hold.

Long distance can be the most ulcer-inducing form of holding. Instead of music, they should just play you the recording of a cash register opening and closing. I once got put on hold while calling from a plane. Not only was this very expensive, it got more expensive because as I was on hold I was flying farther and farther away from my callee.

I suffered a brand-new indignity recently. The phone rang. I picked it up and said, "Hello." A voice said, "Hold, please." Before I could interject, yet another version of "Born to Run" started, a new one featuring maracas. I decided to use my husband's latest toy—his speaker phone. I put the receiver down and listened to the music, which left me free to mambo. I mamboed up a sweat, trying to suppress my homicidal tendencies, and when my phone partner came back to resume the conversation, I said hello again. (I'm quite an ad-libber.)

"Are you on a speaker phone?" she asked.

Naked Beneath My Clothes

"*Sí,*" I replied. (I'd mamboed so hard by this time, I was slightly bilingual.)

She said, "I hate speaker phones. Aren't I important enough to you for you to pick up the receiver?"

I struck back, this time in my native tongue, with, "Aren't I important enough to you not to be left on hold long enough to absorb another culture?"

We reviewed our relationship and decided the answer was a mutual no. We won't be talking again, out of respect for each other's time and also because it had been a wrong number.

23. It's Not Over Even When It's Over

When I was single I had a steadfast rule concerning relationships: "The time you spend grieving over a man should never exceed the amount of time you actually spent with him." In all my years of singledom, I never once obeyed this rule. In fact, I once spent months getting over someone I'd never even met. All right, I was in the sixth grade and he was in the Monkees, but it established a pattern nonetheless.

When I was living in New York City, I was introduced to my first boyfriend through friends of friends. I know these fix-up things rarely work out, but this was no exception. On our first date, we discovered that he lived one block away from me. This is the point at which I should have run.

I'll now tell you my second steadfast rule that I have never followed: "Never get involved with someone who lives near you or works with you." This will double or, in most cases, triple the mourning period because you will see him every day and remember the good time.

In discussing the buildings we lived in, we discovered that we both lived in high rises. He called me when he got home to ask me which way my apartment faced. Lord of lords, it faced his. This is the point at which I should have moved. I did have the presence of mind to suggest that he move, to which he replied, "I was here first." The ring of maturity in his voice should have told me something. It told me nothing.

"Look out of the window," he said. "I'm wearing a red shirt and waving a white handkerchief."

I looked out the window, and there he was. This was the point at which I should have jumped. I counted twelve floors from the top. I wasn't even involved with him yet and I knew the hell that lay before me. He, of course, was thrilled. All he could see was the fun that lay ahead. Why can't men ever sense doom? Why does it have to be right on top of them before they know?

I was a little premature with my doom. Things went pretty well for about a year. I'd come home and the phone would be ringing; I'd look across and see him standing there talking to me. It was kind of a short-distance picture phone, and it was perfect. He was close enough so that I could make sure he was alone, and I far away enough so that I didn't have to put on makeup. If I forgot something at his apartment or visa-versa, there was no trudging across town, no getting stuck in traffic. I was very happy, except that deep down, deep down, I knew. They don't call me the anti-Pollyanna for nothing. I knew that someday my beautiful one-bedroom apartment with a park view was going to be as comfortable as being nailed to a stake.

Then, it happened. We had a big fight about something or other, and we broke up. Our relationship was over, and neither one of us was moving. I resolved never to look out the window of the apartment I paid double for because of the view. I repositioned my couch to face a wall. I would be made of steel; across the street and twelve floors down was dead to me; the window did not exist; I would never again turn around. The first week alone I turned around so many times, I actually lost weight in my neck.

To be fair, it must have been difficult for him too because we got back together three or four times to try to make it work. Anyone who lives in New York City will tell you a good apartment is even harder to find than a good relationship. So, all in all, it took another three years to end. One year in, three years to get out. Triple the time I had allotted. I set out not to make the same mistake again and better my average.

My next boyfriend was a doctor who lived crosstown. This one wasn't my fault. We'd been seeing each other for two years when he got transferred to the hospital across the street. Two years in, three years to get out. I was a lot older and a little closer to my goal.

Then, I really sinned. I don't know how I did something this stupid. I got involved with someone who actually lived *in my building*. I didn't even go into this relationship with doom. I thought it was fate. We'd lived in the same building for ten years and never met and then found each other in the elevator. All I can say is fate, shmate, and this was definitely shmate. I did, however, get very close to my goal. One year in, one and a half years to get out.

This time, though, I really got out. I moved to California. Although I did love New York City, I was unable to look out the window, cross the street, or get in an elevator without running smack into the memories of the ones from whom I got away.

The next man I got involved with lived in Australia, and as real fate would have it, he turned out to be my husband. So I guess the moral of this story is, "Only get involved with men who live on different continents." It's a pain; if you forget something at your apartment, you have to trudge across the Pacific . . . but it eventually works out.

24. The Frequent Flyer Flummox

Frequent flyer miles are a brilliant idea. If you travel all the time for a living and build up thousands of miles, you get a free trip. This is just what someone who travels all the time for a living wants to do with their time off. It's like giving a garbage person who has completed several thousand successful runs a free ride on the truck.

Still, because there are some places that are tempting and because I suffer from missoufreea-phobia (the fear of missing out on something that I might be able to get for free), I belong to every frequent flyer club known to man. I have and will always have just under the amount of miles it takes to get me any place I want to go.

One day, while going through my millions of statements, I thought I had enough miles to get my husband and me two round-trip first-class tickets to London. Ha. It turned out that I had some of my miles on the old program, and the rest of my miles were on the new program. I had just enough miles on each program to get me to the middle of the ocean.

"What if you combine the miles on the old program with the miles on the new program?" I suggested, knowing but not wanting to know the answer.

"I'm sorry, but we're not allowed to do that," the airline operator chirped cheerily.

"Why?" I pleaded.

"I'll go check," she chirped.

"No, no, don't go check." It was too late, I was on hold listening to a watered-down version of Bruce Springsteen (see essay number 22). I began to subtract from my age. She came back on the line.

"I asked my supervisor and she said, 'Just because.' "

"That's good enough for me," I said. The supervisor was obviously a star on the debating team, and I was no match.

"I checked, and you do have enough miles for two round-trip first-class tickets to Skokie."

"That's very kind of you and at the same time very unhelpful. I want to go on vacation, I don't want to do time. What if I purchased two economy tickets to London? Do I have enough miles to get an upgrade?"

Born in the U.S.A., born in the U.S.A., I'm a long, tall daddy, something something something something . . .

She came back on the line.

"Yes. You have enough miles for an upgrade."

"Halleluja, praise the Lord," I wailed.

"All you have to do is purchase two full-fare economy tickets to London."

"How much is full economy fare to London?" I asked, knowing that I had wailed prematurely.

"One thousand eight hundred dollars."

Rita Rudner

"Each?"

"Each."

"How much is the cheapest economy fare to London?"

"Two hundred and fifty dollars."

"Two hundred and fifty dollars? Any swimming involved?" I asked playfully, with the barest note of irritation in my voice.

"No," she replied coldly.

"So, let me get this straight. If I use my money-saving miles, I can spend five times more than I would have spent without them?"

"You get upgraded," she reminded me.

"Yes, that's right. For a mere fifteen hundred dollars more I can get a better bad steak and a wider seat next to a rich person who snores. Forget London. How about New York?"

"Yes, we can give you two round-trip first-class tickets to New York at any time except during the blackout periods."

"When are they?" I asked in a beaten manner.

"With the old miles or the new miles?"

"I don't care."

"I'll check."

Ooooo, oooo, oooo, I'm on fire, oooo, oooo, oooo, I'm on fire . . .

"With the old miles, the blackout periods include any holidays or any good weather."

"And with the new miles?"

"The same."

"Good. I'm glad you checked them both. So that leaves what?" I bleated. I had never bleated before.

"You can go for free any time in August or February."

"Have you ever been to New York in August?"

"No."

"Picture garbage roasting in a sauna and add a sprinkling of gunplay and I think you get the general idea. For a mental picture of February, just freeze the garbage. Forget New York. What about Los Angeles? Wait a second. I live in Los Angeles. What about Hawaii?"

I would not give up.

"Maui, Honolulu, Oahu, or the big island?" she asked mechanically.

"Hold on," I chirped. I sang a little Barry Manilow. I knew where I wanted to go, I just felt like singing. "Oh, Mandy. You came and you gave without . . . I'm back. Maui."

"Fine. You do realize these will be coach and it will be in the rainy season?"

"I don't care. Attach me to the wing and drop me into a volcano, just get me to Hawaii."

"What's your husband's name?"

"Martin Bergman."

"Your name is Rudner and his name is Bergman?"

"Yes, we're in the 1990s or maybe by now the 2000s."

"We'll need proof of your marriage."

"Fine."

"Will you be sending your marriage certificate?"

"No, my in-laws. I'm sorry to get stroppy, but I've been on the phone so long, I've developed an ear infection. Send me two tickets for February, twentieth to the twenty-fourth. February is bad weather, isn't it?"

"Yes, but you have to stay over a Saturday."

"Why?" I exploded. "What is it with the pilots? Why won't they fly on Saturdays? Is there some kind of airline superstition? Do they have dates? Do they like to watch 'The Golden Girls'? Just forget it. Keep my miles and I'll send you my phone bill. I'll stay home for my vacation. I travel all the time anyway."

"All right, but be aware on the new program your miles expire on January eleventh."

I gave up. My missoufreea-phobia kicked in. "Two tickets to Skokie, please."

Rita Rudner

matic. (Someone, somewhere, at a network is going to read this and bring it up at a meeting as a new and exciting idea.)

Attention spans are getting so short it's a little frightening. People don't even read books anymore. They just like short, funny essays where the subject changes every three pages. Just think of me as a literary Ed Sullivan.

Now, my remote control is a way of life. When I stay in a hotel that hasn't updated its television and I have to get up to change the channel, I can see why my parents had me.

As addicted as I am to the television and the remote control, my husband is worse. Once when I was going out of town our electricity was out. My husband didn't care that there were no lights or that all of our food was melting; he just sat in front of the television pressing the remote-control button with tears in his eyes and making a clicking noise with his tongue.

If there was a remote-control Olympics, my husband would easily win it. He can flick through our fifty channels faster and more often than anyone I've ever seen. We can watch a football game, a sitcom, and a war all at the same time. Often, I'm not sure which is which.

A television executive once told me that the important thing was to hook people in right away. A sitcom uses a laugh track so that even if you yourself are not laughing, you are hearing someone thinking it's funny, so you consider giving the show a few more seconds. What can a drama do, though, where viewers have to get to know the characters? When Ann-Margret or Raquel Welch or another one of those beautiful women who are determined to look ugly and play abused come on and say, "My daddy beat me, and my daddy's daddy beat me, and sure as hell no daddy man is ever going to beat me again," what about a sob track? As they take their raggedy children away we could hear peo-ple blowing their noses; that way we'll know it's dra-

Beverly Hills Beggar.

26. Clothes Make the Woman

My husband has a very simple rule for shopping for clothes. If there is something he wants to buy in a store window, he goes in and tries it on. If he doesn't like it, he leaves. He figures, "They put their best clothes in the window; if I don't like them, why even bother looking at the rest of the merchandise?" He leaves with the confidence of knowing that there was nothing else he could have possibly wanted in that store. If I ever walked out of a store without looking at absolutely every item, I would have nightmares similar in intensity to those of a Nazi war criminal. I have to hunt. If there was water in the store, I would have to fish.

It took me about two and a half years of marriage to convince my husband that he needed a new suit. I had to bring the subject up very subtly so as not to appear critical. One day we were walking down the street and I said casually so there was not a possibility in the world that he could take it personally, "Isn't that a nice suit in the window?"

My husband said, "You don't like the way I dress?"

"I didn't say that, I just said that was a nice suit."

"What's wrong with the suit I have?"

"Nothing, nothing at all. It's a fine suit," I lied.

"It's clean."

Rita Rudner

"It's more than clean, it's shiny. When we're out together I don't have to carry a mirror to fix my makeup, I can see myself in your suit."

"So what you're saying is, I need a new suit?"

"That is what I am saying."

We had begun to do a David Mamet play on the street.

"I'll get a new suit."

It was easy, just a few moments of discomfort and he would be trying on clothes . . . so then why was he walking past the store?

"Why are you walking past the store?"

"I'll buy a new suit, I just don't want to buy it now."

"What's wrong with now?"

"We're in New York, I'll buy a new suit when we're home."

"Why, when we're inches from a store and have nothing else to do, do you want to wait 'til we're miles away from a store and very busy?"

"Don't push me. I said I'll buy a suit, and I'll buy a suit."

About six months later I dragged him bodily into a store with the help of a tranquilizer gun and a net. As long as I'm on the subject of men's clothes, why, when they buy an expensive suit, do they get free alterations? When I buy an expensive dress and it has to be taken in or, Heaven forbid, let out, I have to pay another seventy-five dollars. If those morons in Washington ever pass the equal rights amendment, it should say, "Equal pay for equal work and free alterations."

Sometimes my husband likes to help me pick out

clothes. He forgets how long it takes me to make a decision about anything. (I got off jury duty by telling them how long it took me to decide whether or not to buy a jacket.) We always have the same argument. I choose clothes that make me look like a nun (see essay number 19), and my husband chooses clothes that make me look like a hooker. We compromise, and that is why on television I usually look like a flamboyant nun. My husband requires only one thing in a women's clothing store, a chair. You should see how happy he gets when he finds a store that has a chair. He sits there with this glazed, "will it be over soon?" expression on his face, and I try on clothes until he starts to cry. I can't help it, I have to be sure that everything in the store looks absolutely horrible on me . . . and then I buy the dress in the window.

27. Don't It Make Your Blue Carpet Brown?

This is a story that is fresh in my mind because it just happened and my husband isn't even speaking to me yet so I can write this story without fear of interruption. I think, when you hear what happened, you will be on my side. How was I supposed to know that a carpet cleaning service I found in the Yellow Pages would turn our blue carpet dark brown? I picked the ad so perfectly. It wasn't too big (I didn't want an arrogant carpet cleaner who thought he was too good for the job), and it wasn't too small (I didn't want a guy showing up with a broom and a bucket). It was about a quarter of a page and it had a drawing of a nice man in a hat who looked happy and proud.

The men who came to clean our carpet were nice enough. They had a machine that looked official and sounded appropriate. They also had a little waiver that we had to sign after they were through, saying that everything was all right and releasing them from any legal responsibility. Everything was all right, until the next morning when the carpet dried. Then it was the opposite of all right. It was all wrong. It was a carpet that looked like it had spent the night in a kennel. Invisible Great Danes had visited us during the night, and what used to be a moderately dirty carpet is now obscene.

Because I come from a family where nothing was ever confronted (my father was a lawyer who didn't like to argue), my solution to this problem is simple enough—buy new carpeting and pretend it didn't happen. That way everyone is happy, and it is good for the economy, which, let's face it, needs a boost. The cleaning people don't get sued, people make money because I have to buy new carpeting, and all it costs me is lots of money. My husband doesn't like this solution. He thinks we should spend our money on things we want, not on things other people have ruined. However, it is my responsibility to handle this situation because I was the one who was irresponsible enough to want to live in a house that had a clean carpet. I called the carpet cleaning service.

Henry answers the phone.

"Hello, Henry speaking."

"Hello, Henry, this is Rita Rudner. You ruined, I mean cleaned, my carpet yesterday, and even though I know you didn't do it on purpose and I don't want you to fire the men who did it, whatever you did turned my blue carpet brown. How can we work together to fix it?"

"There is nothing we put in our cleaning solution that could turn a blue carpet brown," he replied helpfully.

"But it is. It has big brown spots all over it."

"Do you have a dog?" he asked.

"No."

"Are you sure? That's what it sounds like to me."

"I don't have a dog, I have a husband . . . and he's housebroken. Is there any place you can recommend that specializes in getting the stains out of carpets?"

"I'll tell you, I had my carpets cleaned and they came up with big ugly spots, too."

"And what did you do about it?"

"I went out and bought new carpet."

"Just out of curiosity, did you use your own machine to clean your carpets?"

"Yup."

"Have people called with this complaint before?"

"Yup."

"Do you think you should buy a new carpet cleaning machine?"

"Nope."

"Thank you very much for your time."

I couldn't do it. I couldn't sue someone to whom God had forgotten to add a brain. I've just had a look at the carpet and the stains seem to be getting lighter. . . . Let me go look at it from the staircase. . . . My mistake—it was just wishful looking. I have a few options here, and none of them are pretty.

1. Buy a big dog and blame it on him.
2. Replace the carpet with a new one while my husband is sleeping.
3. Buy so much furniture you are unaware that a carpet even exists.

Or

4. *Look in the Yellow Pages under "Carpet Stain Remover Specialist."*

Because I can't be trusted, I choose number four. I look at the ads even more carefully; this time I will not be fooled. I pick a big ad, the biggest ad on the page: "Carpet Stain Remover Specialists." I dial the number. They answer.

"Hello, Henry speaking."

I hang up. I have to go now. I'm buying a dog.

28. Everything I've Ever Learned I've Never Had to Know Again

Most people can look back at their years in school and pick out a teacher who really influenced them in their later life, a teacher who took time out of their schedule and helped them above and beyond the call of duty. I hope I'm unique, because looking back at my scanty, and I do mean scanty, education, I never had a teacher I didn't want to run over. Okay, I know that's a little harsh . . . back over. Okay, dent.

A lot of it was my fault. I was a headstrong kid who wanted to be a dancer. School was standing in the way of my career. I felt it was a waste of my time and my legs, so I can't really blame teachers for my disinterest, but I will anyway. I have very little recollection of what went on in school, because I graduated high school when I was fifteen and never looked back, but here's all I remember and what I think I learned.

First grade: Mrs. Argyle. She did teach me to read and loved to make us line up for things—I feel this prepared me for boarding airplanes and lining up at the bank, movies, etc. While I wait, I can read a newspaper.

Second grade: Mrs. Flug. She failed to recognize that I

Official graduation photo.

Rita Rudner

had my hand up and had to go to the bathroom. Very disturbing results. This taught me never to ask permission to perform bodily functions.

Third grade: Mrs. McCorckle. Nothing.

Fourth grade: Mrs. Somerstein. She wore gingham dresses; this taught me never to wear gingham after age forty.

Fifth grade: Miss Chrissy. She had short blond hair and wore very short skirts with very high heels, and she dated the gym teacher. This taught me I would never be someone who could attract a gym teacher.

Sixth grade: Mr. Fannell. He was very bald and sweaty and had buckteeth and loved math. Through careful observation in the library while I should have been studying, I learned that people who looked like Mr. Fannell could never attract people who looked like Miss Chrissy.

My seventh-grade teacher, Miss Mickie, taught a very difficult class called "home room." Miss Mickie's class was the class we had to sit in before we went to the other classes where people had to try to teach us something. Essentially, Miss Mickie had to take roll call to find out who was there that day. She was not qualified. Miss Mickie couldn't remember who was who. We would call out "Here" indiscriminately, and she would mark it on her little sheet. Miss Mickie eventually went potty. Every morning our principal would read a thought for the day over the school loudspeaker. Miss Mickie would answer him. We didn't know whether to tell the principal that she had slipped into another dimension or try to explain to Miss Mickie the concept of

Naked Beneath My Clothes

a sound system. We eventually decided to graduate and let next year's class deal with it.

Eighth grade: Mr. Pickle. What I learned from him was quite important; I learned that if you want to be a teacher, you cannot have a name like Mr. Pickle. I also learned that being an eighth-grade teacher did not mean that you were through having skin problems, and I learned that I could not dissect a frog without throwing up.

Ninth grade: Mrs. Camolie. She had the lowest bosoms in the world. Without knowing it, she mentally prepared me for the possibility of eventually having very low bosoms.

Tenth grade: Mr. Rodrieguez. He was my algebra teacher, and although he was a very smart man, he had a very thick Spanish accent that I could barely understand. I was already at the end of a cliff where math was concerned, and his accent was the perfect thing to kick me over the edge. From Mr. Rodrieguez, I learned the importance of a scapegoat.

Eleventh and twelfth grades: I did these two grades together to be able to enter the dance world professionally a year younger. I don't remember teachers as much as I remember kids smoking an assortment of things in the bathrooms. I also remember lots of different teachers getting very angry and dragging kids out of bathrooms. I remember being afraid to go into the bathrooms. From this I learned the importance of having your own bathroom.

That was the end of school for me, and in a way I did learn from my teachers. They just didn't know what they taught me.

Rita Rudner

The Concerned Cows.

29. Things That Sound Better Than They Are

1. Hot buttered rum.
2. Staying home with a good book.
3. The Super Bowl.
4. Picnics.
5. The beach.
6. Pâté.
7. Traveling.
8. Cherry pie.
9. Face lifts.
10. Being a princess.

30. Things That Are Better Than They Sound

5

1. Elvis Costello.
2. Liver.
3. Buses.
4. Foreign films.
5. Volvos.
6. Rhubarb.
7. The ballet.
8. V-8 Juice.
9. Documentaries.
10. Las Vegas.

Naked Beneath My Clothes

31. Driving Each Other Crazy

If my husband and I are going to get into an argument, it usually happens in the car. A car is a very small place where you can scrutinize each other's every movement. I think we need a bigger car. I think we need a two-bedroom car, or at least one with a cement wall down the middle.

I have been driving for five years now. I learned how when I moved from New York to L.A. In New York you don't have to know how to drive, you just have to know how to jump out of the way of taxis, which are for some reason speeding along the sidewalks. Taxi drivers in New York are seldom aware of a change of surface. They are barely aware of what country they are in. In London, if you want to be a taxi driver, you have to study for years and take an extensive test called "the knowledge" before you are granted a license. In New York, if you want to be a taxi driver, you have to have a foot.

Whenever my husband and I are in my car and I am driving, he is convinced that I am out to kill us both. He has no confidence in my ability to stop. Every time we come up to a red light I see him gripping the side of the car as if he were hanging on to the outside of a speeding train.

Rita Rudner

"Christ, brake, stop . . . stop, there's a red light!" he bellows.

"I know there's a red light, that's why I'm slowing down. That's what I do right before I stop. I use it as a kind of preparation. I tried speeding up as a preparation for a while, but it made stopping more difficult," I say, trying not to speed up for spite.

"You have such a heavy foot!"

"I don't have a heavy foot. I have lots of other things that are heavy, but my foot is just right."

I don't get it. When I leave in the car on my own he never thinks it's the last time he's going to see me. If he thinks I drive as badly as he obviously thinks I drive, then why does he let me drive at all? If I need to get somewhere, why doesn't he just put me in a sack and call a cab?

My husband is convinced that he is a much safer driver than I am. He has two moving violations, I have none. When he came over from England, we had a huge fight because I told him you had to stop at stop signs, whether someone is coming the other way or not, and he didn't believe me. Evidently they don't have to stop in England. He didn't have time to explain that to the officer. He refused to go to traffic school, where you can get your ticket erased and you can actually learn the rules of another country, so the next officer had to tell him about double yellow lines. Did you know that you can make a U-turn at will in England? One day we were driving along a busy street and all of a sudden he made the most beautiful U-turn right in front of a police car. The policeman flashed his lights and my husband waved; he thought the officer was complimenting him on completing such a pretty turn in such heavy traffic. Instead he was introduced to ticket number two.

And yet I've never once thought that my husband was going to kill me in the car. I had confidence in his ability to drive long before he knew any of the rules. That's why, when we go on trips, he drives and I am left with the unhappy experience of trying to read the map. Because I learned how to drive so late in life, I do not have a very developed sense of map. Very often I will sit in the car and stare at it silently for hours, just hoping that something will magically begin to make sense to me. My husband says we would have a better chance of getting to our destination if he just taped the map on the windshield and drove by feel.

In our travels, we have gone into many countries unnecessarily . . . and without our passports . . . and without the correct currency. My indisputable talent is my ability, no matter where we are, to find cows. It doesn't matter if we are going sight-seeing in Germany or to the theater in Pasadena, you give me the map and I will lead you to cows. If only cows could talk and tell us how to get back on the 101.

I am now going to solve our problem; since I'm a safe driver, and he's good at reading maps, why don't we reverse responsibilities? We tried that once, and he was so concentrated on reading the map, he forgot to panic at every red light, my heavy foot remembered to brake, and it just didn't feel right. We missed the screaming . . . and the cows. So for now, we'll keep our roles . . . and look for a two-bedroom car.

Rita Rudner

Rita finds cows.

32. I'm Just Not an Inn Person

My husband and I decided to get away from the kids for a couple of days. This was very hard to do since we don't actually have kids, but we didn't let that stop us. We figured we might have kids someday, and we would certainly want to get away from them. We would use this as a practice run.

I found a book of weekend getaways and discovered somewhere idyllic. Not one of those chain hotels that look like they were built with giant Lego, but a small, intimate, personal establishment where every room is named and furnished differently. It was driving distance too because flying with my husband is so stressful I would rather be with the kids. We set out on our journey, which was only a two-hour drive from Los Angeles, and due to my expert map reading, a mere four and a half hours and two hundred cows later, we were there. (If this is confusing you, please see essay number 31.)

We pulled up to a . . . I'm not sure how to describe it . . . it wasn't a house, and it certainly wasn't a hotel . . . it was kind of a fancy shack. I knew I should have been suspicious when I made the reservation and they didn't want a credit card number, they just trusted me. There was no bellperson, so my husband had to lug our suitcase up to the check-in desk. This is the conversation that we have whenever my husband picks up a suitcase that I have packed.

HIM: What the hell did you put in here, rocks?

ME: Do you want to pack next time?

HIM: (Grumble noises.)

We walked in and there were antiques everywhere. There was even one standing behind the registration desk waiting to check us in. He had obviously been a fixture of the place for years. (It's the history of these places that makes them so special.)

He said, "Welcome, to the Inn on the Lake. I'm Jerome. If there is anything I can do for you, please don't hesitate to ask."

We paid two hundred dollars in cash because they didn't take credit cards, and Jerome walked us around the corner.

"This is the dining room," he announced proudly.

There was just one big table that sat about ten people.

"Are there any tables for two?" my husband asked. (My husband is slightly less social than Salman Rushdie.)

"No, we're just one big happy family here. Everyone who stays at the Inn on the Lake eats at the same table."

"We'll have room service tonight," my husband whispered to me.

"There's no room service at the Inn on the Lake,"

Jerome cautioned. He might have been old, but he still had his hearing. "The kitchen closes at nine o'clock."

We had rented the penthouse with the ocean view at the Inn on the Lake. As we started up the creaky stairs, Jerome said, "I'll take your suitcase. It doesn't matter about my back."

My husband carried the suitcase up the four flights, and we arrived at the Irving Gull suite.

"Who was Irving Gull?" my husband wheezed.

"Don't know," Jerome said. "I just started working here yesterday."

Jerome opened the door. It was a beautiful room. A four-poster bed with a blue Laura Ashley–print comforter, antique bureau, and lace curtains. It was almost as nice as the guest room we have in our house that we never go into. All for only two hundred dollars.

"Where's the view of the ocean?" I asked.

Jerome pointed out the window. "Right over there, past all of those roof antennas."

I looked, and looked a little bit harder, and there it was, the view of the ocean. It was an excellent view of the ocean, too . . . if you were Michael Jordan.

Jerome stared at us. We tipped Jerome and he left. Quaint, rustic, peaceful, quiet, romantic, these are all the words they used to describe the Inn on the Lake. You have to read between the lines in these brochures. What they were really saying was that the Inn on the Lake did not have a television. We are not people who should ever be without a television.

Rita Rudner

It was very sad. My husband sat in bed staring at the spot he thought the television should be.

"We could go down and eat with the strangers," I said. There was no response. "We could stand on the bed and look at the ocean." Still nothing. "We could forfeit our two hundred dollars and be back home for 'The Tonight Show.'"

I've never seen anyone move like that. He moved faster than a postal worker when it's time for lunch.

He left me to give the keys back to Jerome and tell him we were leaving. I didn't really know what to tell him; I didn't want to insult the place, so I just told him the truth. We were just about to unpack and we got terribly homesick. We missed the kids.

"Just tell me where I parked my car."

Rita Rudner

33. Daddy Dearest

My father raised me with an incredible fear of becoming chilly. From the time I was very young I remember being forced to take a sweater to school. I lived in Miami and went to a school that did not have air-conditioning. To this day I take sweaters to the beach, to summer picnics, and to saunas. Even as I write this, I have a sweatshirt thrown over my shoulders. The temperature outside is 103 degrees, inside with my overworked air conditioner it is about 87 degrees, but you never know, there could be a draft.

This happened before I was old enough to recall; my mother told me that when I was an infant, my father read somewhere that babies could strangle themselves, so even though I was too young to get out of the crib and the curtains were across the room, he made sure all the curtain strings were tied in bows so I couldn't reach them. When I was older I was not allowed to have any nightgown that had strings just in case I twisted and it accidentally turned into a noose during the night. I still have a fear of drawstrings.

This is ingrained on my psyche. The first day of junior high school I had brand new shoes, and I was made to wear socks so I wouldn't get blisters. The one thing a popular kid does not do is wear socks. I took them off during the first class and felt much better, but by the end of the day I had blisters. I still wear socks, and I'm still not popular.

All the time I was growing up I was convinced we were rich. After all, it isn't just anyone who gets to live by the railroad tracks. We got to hear the trains go by two or three times a day! I was convinced we were rich because my father always tried to get me anything I wanted. I wanted an accordion, he bought me an accordion. (I should have left the socks on, they would have looked perfect with the accordion.) It wasn't until years later that he let it slip that he had convinced the salesman to buy it on time. One dollar a week. If I had known that I would have practiced. I still feel guilty whenever I see a marching band.

Another reason I thought we were rich was that all the other kids got a weekly allowance. I was made to ask for how much money I thought I needed for the week. If I had money left over, I didn't ask for money the next week, but if I needed a few more dollars, he gave them to me, no questions asked. I have never been able to stick to a budget because I don't know how to figure out exactly what constitutes a budget. I just know I should have more money coming in than going out. In this area I'm doing better than the government.

When I wanted a dog, he got me a fish. When the fish died, he got me a turtle. When the turtle drowned, he got me a bird. When the bird flew out the window, he got me a dog. Can you imagine that? I killed three different species,

Rita Rudner

The accordion my father bought
me. He hadn't paid for the "I" yet.

and he still granted my dog wish. He even let me name it. I had a German shepherd named Tiny. (I didn't kill my dog; she died eleven years later of natural causes.)

I was in a department store with my parents, and I saw an enormous pink, stuffed pig. I really wanted that pig, and my father said, "No. You already have more stuffed animals than a taxidermist." I didn't know what that meant, but I understood the no part. A few weeks later I came down with the measles, and he surprised me by coming home from work with the pig. This has rubbed off on my adult life and affected my relationship with my husband. When I get sick, I want a present.

My father always thought I was capable of doing anything I wanted to do, he always trusted me, and he always did everything he could do to help me through whatever particular trauma I was going through at the time. Even before I could read about all of the things that go on out there, I knew I was very lucky. What your parents think of you does affect how you feel about yourself for the rest of your life. I'm putting my sweatshirt on now. It's down to 82 degrees. I'm feeling a little chilly.

34. Things That Never Caught On

1. Baby toupees.
2. Reversible shoes.
3. Black toothpaste.
4. Fish leashes.
5. Chocolate plant food.
6. Collapsible crutches.
7. High-heeled sneakers.
8. Cow sushi.
9. Bulimic Barbie.
10. Wooden suspenders.

35. If I Live in a Fantasy World, Why Do I Have to Pay Taxes?

With a visit from the same luck fairy who visits teenagers who get pregnant the first time they have sex, I got audited the first time I ever filed. No one ever really prepared me for the paperwork that accompanies adulthood. Someone in the show I was in had mentioned that you had to save receipts and take them to an accountant before April 15. I kept them all in a big shoebox and brought them to an accountant on the fourteenth. They were in no particular order. I just dumped them on the accountant's desk and expected him to do something magical.

He said, "You haven't put these receipts in categories and added them up?"

I said, "Isn't that your job?" I sounded like a smart aleck, but I really thought that's what accountants did.

He said, "Why don't you go home and put these in little piles and add them up?"

I said, "Because I'm a dancer. If I could put things in little piles and add them up, I'd be an accountant."

I can still see the hatred in his eyes. I sat in the outer office and made little receipt piles for hours. I added them up to the best of my more than limited ability because I didn't have a calculator and I thought if I asked him for his, he might hit me. I gave him a sheet of numbers I had partially made up, and a few weeks later he sent me papers to sign and send in. Since I'd been on the road for almost a year and I had quite a few deductions, a few months later I got a five-hundred-dollar refund from the government. I thought, "This is good."

I spent the five hundred dollars frivolously on food and rent, and one day a letter arrived from the IRS. I didn't really understand it, something about going downtown on June 12 and bringing my records. I thought, "Maybe the IRS is inviting me to some sort of party and they wanted me to provide the music." I called my accountant and told him about my letter. There was a long silence and he said, "I'm too busy to help you. Bring all the receipts you brought to me down to the IRS and act innocent."

Act innocent? Innocent of what? I called one of my friends and told her what had happened.

"You're going down yourself? You're not even bringing a lawyer?" she gasped.

"Why would I need a lawyer? I haven't done anything wrong," I said innocently.

"Well, you've got the innocent act down," she said.

On the twelfth of June I took the subway to Rectum Street or whatever it was called, took a number, and sat in the waiting room with all of my shoeboxes. Sweat was in the air. There were lots of nervous people sitting around me holding their numbers. I didn't blame them for being nervous. I'd be nervous too if I didn't have shoeboxes. I was confident that eveything was going to be all right, although the sobbing noises that were coming from behind the dirty glass doors were not comforting.

Finally my number was called. I stood up and said, "I'll have a half a pound of very lean roast beef and some potato salad." I got a laugh in the auditing room at the IRS. (This was a sign that ten years later I would become a comedian.) I walked into the little cubbyhole of the poor bespectacled little man who had been assigned to my case and put all of my shoeboxes on his desk.

He said, "Why did you bring me shoes?"

I said, "These are my receipts." I opened the boxes, and because of the subway journey and because I had not stapled any of the piles together, they were back in their original state of chaos.

We sat there for eight hours. This guy was thorough. He was so thorough, he found some mistakes. He found a whole pile of receipts that were deductions I had forgotten to include. There were sobbing noises coming from my cubbyhole and they weren't coming from me. At the end of the audit, the IRS owed me two hundred dollars.

I wish I could say I've gotten better at paperwork through the years, but all I can say is that I no longer use shoeboxes to hold my receipts. I've switched to paper bags.

Rita Rudner

36. When in Doubt, Make It Up

I'm ashamed to say I've always loved makeup. I know that a woman's self-worth isn't wrapped up in how she looks, but even cavewomen rubbed berry juice on their cheeks. They must have known something. I walk into a department store, and the acres of overpriced items and women who know how to use them are somehow comforting to me. I am confident that every product I buy is going to totally transform me into the girl in the picture, and even though it doesn't, the momentary fantasy is worth the money. It must be, otherwise we would sue. Imagine millions of women showing up in court saying, "I spent three hundred dollars on this stuff and not one person stopped me on the street and said, 'Excuse me, are you Isabella Rossellini?' I want my money back."

I do get a little upset when I'm walking through a store and a lab-coated "beauty expert" says, "Makeover for you today?" I usually spend a good fifteen minutes in the morning using my potions, preparations, and concoctions with great care and skill, and here is a total stranger practically screaming at me in public, "You look horrible!"

For a Christmas gift one year, a friend gave me a certificate for a facial and makeover in an exclusive salon. I didn't know whether to thank her or demand an explanation. I thanked her and made the appointment. I sat in the waiting room with lots of women who had more money than I did. You can always tell if people are rich by looking at their shoes. If they're rich, their shoes look like they've been worn maybe two or three times and polished in between each wearing. My shoes always look like I have been doing farm work.

When my turn came I was ushered into a small dark room by a woman from a Slavic country. I lay down and Svetallaninintanova shone a bright light in my face and inspected my pores.

"Oh, dear," she said. "You have never had a facial before, have you?"

"No, I've been busy trying to earn a living," I wanted to say, but didn't.

"This looks very bad. This will take a few treatments," she warned.

She then stuck my face over a pot of boiling water and left me in the room for twenty minutes. When Svetallaninintanova returned, she hosed me down and smeared my face with thick white paste and left me to harden. When it felt like I was wearing a hockey mask, she reappeared.

"How you doing?" she asked brightly.

"I'm having fun now, you bitch," I answered, knowing that since I could not move my mouth she would be unable to decipher my words. She removed the plaster by dunking my head in warm water. I lay back down.

"Now the bitch go to work on your pores," she said.

I was in big trouble. She pinched and poked me for an hour. And what did I do at the end of it all to get even? I tipped her. I slammed five dollars in her hand and said, "Take that!"

I was then shuffled to the makeover room and was forced to look into a mirror to see what Svetallaninintanova had done to me. I looked like I had walked into a wasp nest.

The makeup lady said, "I see you had Svetallaninintanova. She does a very deep cleaning. Don't worry, we'll cover all that up."

She then proceeded to fill in all the pores that had been so thoroughly purified. Because I was partially in a state of shock and I didn't understand what they were saying, I agreed to buy every product they had used on me. My certificate was for one hundred and twenty-five dollars; I owed them two hundred and fifty.

When I came home I asked my husband, "Notice anything different about me?"

He said, "Did you walk into a wasp nest?"

He always knows how to make me feel better. The phone rang, and it was the salon. They said, "You forgot to make another appointment. When do you want to come again?"

I said, "When Elizabeth Taylor marries a truck driver."

I have to call now and make another appointment.

Naked Beneath My Clothes

It's for this muscle here."

Rita Rudner

37. Rethinking Chapter 31

My husband has asked me to add this chapter. Remember when I told you that I was a much better driver than he was? Well, I just had my first car accident, and what a charming experience it was. Of course the important thing is that no one was hurt, but once that's established the fun begins.

Because I live in Los Angeles, where car insurance is both mandatory and unobtainable, I was involved in an accident with people who had no insurance. Luckily, I'm insured for that. But in checking the fine print on my policy, not for collision. Not for collision? What am I insured for . . . near misses?

First of all, this whole thing happened because my husband's fancy car was in the shop while a team of experts were continuing to look for the invisible mariachi band that we hear every time we go over thirty miles an hour. We were on the way to pick up his car, and I signaled to turn left and foolishly failed to see that the car behind the car behind me was going too fast. I went to turn, the car behind me went around me and continued, and the car behind him smashed into me.

While we waited for the police, the two men who ran

into me told me that the accident was my fault for trying to turn left where it was legal to turn left. When I told them I thought it was their fault for not stopping or going around me, they decided it was the car behind me's fault. If the car behind me had possessed the decency to run into me, they would have avoided me.

The police arrived, and all I can say is that Zsa Zsa had a point. If you were a policeman and had been called to the scene of an accident, wouldn't you ask what happened to cause the accident? So would I. When my husband tried to tell the policeman, he screamed very loudly, "Shut up, buddy!" We had all seen the Rodney King video, so no one spoke after that.

The policeman then asked if I had insurance. I gave him my card. He asked the other people if they had insurance. They said, "We're not sure." The policeman said, "I'm going to have to issue you a warning. You should go get insurance." This is the best part. The policeman then gave me the name, phone number, and address of the people who hit me and gave them my name, phone number, and address and said, "I'm not filing a report, work it out between yourselves." Then he left. What if one of us wanted to work it out by beating one of the other ones up? I guess he figured we weren't worth the paperwork, but if one of us got killed, he would come write it up.

I'm very lucky because these were nice people who offered to pay my damages if I wouldn't sue them, and they're very lucky because I'm not going to sue them because I

Rita Rudner

won't get any money back and it will raise my insurance rates. The policeman is very lucky because I was so scared of him I forgot to get his name and badge number, and my husband is very lucky because he now has proof that he is the better driver.

Suzie's new Nike Pump Bra was a huge success.

Rita Rudner

38. Nightmare on Sixty-fourth Street

To show you what a nice person I am, I have decided to tell you about the night I baby-sat for my friend's three-year-old daughter and her unhousebroken puppy who was in heat. My friend had been called away on a family emergency, and her husband was out of town on business, so "Aunt Rita" got the phone call. I had always said I would baby-sit or dog-sit anytime. I just hadn't imagined doing them simultaneously.

I arrived at my friend's house to pick up her two most prized possessions—her daughter (I use the word *possession* at my own risk because even at three the child was saying, "You not the boss of my life") and her bichon frise (I'm sure at one point I saw that on a menu). She put the dog in a box and said, "She goes on papers in the kitchen. Please don't let her on the street. In this condition she'll mate with anything, and she's so young that if she gets pregnant, she could die. Here are her doggie diapers; you can put them on when you take her out of the box."

I left with doggie box in one hand and the child in the other and faced my first hurdle: hailing a taxi without letting go of either one of them. We took the bus.

The little girl was happy and not missing her mother

yet, so she started to sing. She started to sing Christmas carols at the top of her lungs. This was fine except the dog in the box started to sing with her, and I wasn't supposed to have a dog on the bus. This caused us to get kicked off the bus and walk the last ten blocks, which caused the little girl to cry and miss her mother. While I was dragging a crying child and a dog in heat down the street, other dogs got a whiff of my dog, and by the time we got to my apartment we were a walking kennel.

We arrived at my very clean apartment and I put sheets down over the rugs and then opened the box. The dog was thrilled to be free. She ran around the apartment like a dog in heat carefully avoiding all of the sheets I had put down. I got the doggie diapers and tried to put them on her. I had a better chance of getting a garter belt on a guppie. The little girl said, "I bored," and started to cry.

"What do you want to do?" I asked.

"Swimming," she replied.

I had mentioned there was a swimming pool in my building when she was a few months old, and she had re-membered. I put down some newspapers in the kitchen, showed them to the dog, said a little prayer, and left. The dog started to bark. I figured she'd stop. She'd either stop or she'd get laryngitis.

Before I let the little girl into the pool, I gave her a short speech. I said, "This is a very grown-up pool. If you have to go to the bathroom, you have to do it now. Do you have to go?"

Rita Rudner

"No."

"Are you sure?"

"Yes."

I played with her in the water for a few minutes, and she got very quiet and a strange look came over her face. I said, "What's the matter?"

She said, "I don't want to talk about it."

I said, "I'm taking you to the bathroom."

She said, "You not the boss of my life," and started to scream.

I then said, "I'll do anything you want me to do for the rest of my life if you'll just stop screaming." Three-year-olds have the lungs of an elephant.

We went back to the apartment and the dog was still barking, but it was a little huskier in tone. She was beginning to sound a little like Debra Winger. I said a little prayer again and opened the door. The dog had indeed gone on the papers.

"Good dog," I said. "Good dog." The dog was so excited she rolled on the papers, and there is no gentle way to say this. She had beautiful long white fluffy ears, and now one of them was decorated with a "chocolate cigar." (I tried to find a gentle way to say it.)

Feeling like Joan Crawford, I started to chase after the dog with a scissors. The dog howled. The child screamed. My neighbors called to see if I was sacrificing a goat. I finally cut the thing out of the dog's ear and got the little girl watching television and, since I had a full night at home in front of me and a laundry room on my floor, decided to wash clothes. I opened the door and put the laundry in the hall. The dog rushed out. I left her there for maybe three seconds and went to the get the little girl. When I came back into the hall, the very young, very small bichon frise was mating with a German shepherd. My neighbor had let her dog out to run in the hall. I pulled them apart and wondered how I was going to explain the puppies. I just decided to stay as still as I could in my apartment and wait for morning.

The phone rang, and it was my girlfriend's husband, who had come back to town early. When he arrived he asked me if everything was all right. I told him, "Yes." I just couldn't say, "In a few months' time your very expensive and very small puppy will die giving birth to Rin-Tin-Tin."

I worried a lot, and when I ran into my neighbor in the hall, I told her what had happened. She said, "Relax. I'm sure everything will be all right."

"How do you know?" I asked. "All it takes is one sperm with ambition."

Luckily she was right; the mating ritual hadn't been completed . . . for a very good reason: her German shepherd was a girl.

Rita Rudner

39. Things That Make My Day

1. Finding a parking space with time left on the meter.
2. Weighing myself and finding that for no particular reason, I have lost two pounds.
3. Discovering ten dollars in a coat pocket.
4. After doing the laundry, finding a mate for every single sock.
5. Going to the dentist and finding that they actually have magazines I want to look at.
6. Finding a letter from a friend in the middle of all the bills and junk mail.
7. Buying makeup and getting a free gift.
8. Finding a great old movie on video that I haven't seen.
9. Anyone giving me a compliment of any kind. (Even when I order something in a restaurant and the waiter says "Good choice," I sit a little taller.)
10. Just remembering that I never have to date again.

40. Cooking His Goose

In the early eighties I was dating someone who really badgered me about cooking. He made me feel like there was something wrong with me because I thought food originated from a menu. We had been seeing each other for a few weeks when it started:

"Why don't you ever cook anything for me?" he asked.

"Because I like you," I said.

"If you like me, why don't you cook anything for me?"

(He wasn't getting my jokes. Always a very bad sign.) This wasn't a financial cry for help on his part, because we were both working and we alternated picking up the check. This was something embedded deep in his childhood. At some point a connection had been made in his brain that welded women to kitchens. He started to buy me cookbooks. I would read a recipe until there was a direction or utensil that I couldn't understand, and then that recipe was dead to me. But I tried. I started with things that you cook in a blender. I graduated from milk shakes to cold soup. He was getting very excited and started to make out fantasy menus that I could one day cook for him. I was asleep one night and the phone rang.

"Hello," I slurred.

"Cornish hens," said the voice on the other end.

"Pardon?"

"You could make Cornish hens. They're easy."

I woke up the next morning and thought, Did I dream about Cornish hens last night? Then the phone rang again.

"Don't forget to stuff them. You have to stuff them with a wild rice mixture that includes mushrooms."

As most people do who are involved in relationships that are marginal, I tried not to tell him to get lost just yet. I gave him the benefit of the doubt and remembered how hard it was to meet someone in New York who wasn't a murderer. This was just a phase. He had good qualities, too . . . he was a nice person . . . he bathed . . . etc., etc.

I decided to do one big dinner for him and maybe then he would shut up. I searched for recipes that I could understand, and when I had them I went to the grocery store with my list. I shopped, schlepped, and chopped. Then I sautéed, steamed, and baked. He was due at seven-thirty. He showed up with roses. This isn't so bad, I thought. I could do this once a year.

He sat himself at the table, and one by one I brought out the masterpieces. Appetizer: mushrooms stuffed with crabmeat. Salad: grapefruit and avocadoes. Main course: Cornish hens stuffed with a wild rice mixture that included mushrooms. Dessert: A Grand Marnier soufflé. Coffee and aperitifs, and I was done. Then something very strange hap-

Naked Beneath My Clothes

pened. He stood up and went over to the couch and turned on the television. I spent at least an hour cleaning up the kitchen, and when I came out he was asleep on the sofa. I woke him up.

"Excuse me. Is there anything else you'll be requiring this evening?" I asked.

"No. That was a wonderful dinner. You're really going to be a great cook. What are you going to make tomorrow night?"

"Tomorrow night?" I replied with venom.

"Lamb chops are easy, too. You'll love to make lamb chops. Don't forget the mint jelly. That's very important."

People who don't get your jokes very often don't notice venom.

"I have to tell you, I don't think we should ever be in the same apartment again." (I figured since we weren't communicating all that well, I should take the blunt approach.)

"Pardon? I thought we were just starting to hit it off," he said. "That was such a great dinner."

"It was. It was a great dinner, and it was something else. It was your last dinner."

I never heard from him again, but I hope he found the human Cuisinart he was looking for. I know some women get enjoyment out of cooking, and that's different. Some women have families, and they don't want their children to starve, and that's different, too. But it's very important to find a man who thinks the same way you do. My husband and I agree that the kitchen is a place to walk through, not

Rita Rudner

to linger. When we do cook, we usually cook together. I do get satisfaction out of making him dinner once in a while. I made him a special one for his birthday last year. I made Cornish hens. With a wild rice mixture that included mushrooms.

41. Things I Hope I Never Have to Say in a Restaurant

1. Waiter, my pepper is moving.
2. All I did was knock the candle over; don't you have insurance?
3. How was I supposed to know the chopsticks had splinters?
4. Duck!!! Spaghetti!!!
5. I make this much better.

42. Fillings . . . Nothing More Than Fillings

There is only one type of person who is more annoying than the type of person who cannot gain weight, and that is the type of person who has never had a filling. I married one. All my life I have brushed, flossed, massaged, and rinsed, and yet I have more silver in my mouth than that guy in the James Bond movies. When I met my husband, he hadn't been to a dentist for ten years. He flossed right before he went, and everything was fine.

This is one area where I feel safe blaming my parents. I inherited their teeth and therefore their struggle. My grandfather had false teeth that he could click in and out of his mouth. He also had allergies. Two things that don't go together are loose false teeth and sneezing. Luckily, he was a good catch.

My husband also has a perfect bite and has never had to have braces. I had teeth that stuck out so far, I used to eat other kids' candy bars by accident. This was my fault because I was a thumb sucker. (I thought I'd just come out and tell you so you don't have to wait for the big exposé in the *Enquirer*.) I had very bad buckteeth. I also had very big teeth and a very small mouth. You'd think that when I

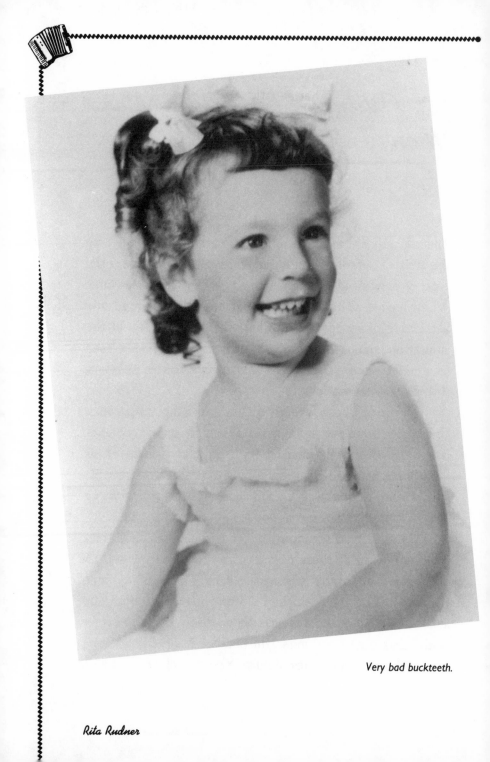

Very bad buckteeth.

Rita Rudner

was getting put together genetically, whoever was in charge of the mouth would have some kind of cross-referencing available to them. I had the teeth of Mary Tyler Moore coupled with the mouth of Bernadette Peters. I had to have eight teeth pulled before my lips could even think about meeting.

My parents didn't tell me I was going to get my teeth pulled because they knew I would react badly. They told me I had to have a filling, and I still reacted badly. They might as well have told me about the pulling. I remember the dentist rolling up my sleeve and giving me a shot in the arm and then waking up on a couch. I never felt a thing. That is how I want to have a baby.

Then came the braces. I wore them for a few years. Then came the retainers. I wore those for a few years, and then came the wisdom teeth that pushed everything out of line again. More pulling. More retainers.

I can't help but wonder why wisdom teeth show up so late in life. Maybe a long time ago teeth were all gone by age twenty and it was God's way of giving you another chance at chewing. If that indeed is the case, somebody should notify God (I'd do it, but I'm busy) that people are living a lot longer these days and what we really need is a third set of teeth. To think that one set of teeth is going to last us from ages six to . . . let's say, eighty-seven is unreasonable. At fifty it should start all over again. They get loose, you put them under the pillow, and the new ones come in. Of course, they should all come out at the same time and the new ones should come in overnight. A toothless fifty-year-old is not nearly as adorable as a toothless five-year-old.

But wouldn't that be great? A set of teeth when you were actually mature enough to take care of them. As it is, the only thing that happens is that your gums start to go. My dentist recently told me to spend more time with my gums.

He said, "It's easy. While you're watching television you just take your toothbrush and massage in between your teeth with the rubber tip." He forgot to add, "It's also attractive."

The first time I brought my rubber tip to an evening of television, my husband said, "What are you doing?"

"I'm massaging my gums with my rubber tip," I said.

"Why on earth are you doing it here?"

"This is where my dentist thought it would be a good idea for me to do it."

"He's a dentist. Maybe in his house this is acceptable behavior. Maybe his whole family watches 'The Tonight Show' with rubber tips hanging out of their mouths. I think it looks disgusting."

I retreated to the bathroom and cursed my parents. A few days later my husband had his annual checkup. It turns out that although he may have a perfect bite and no cavities, his gums are retreating faster than General Custer. So now he's changed his mind; he thinks we look cute watching television together while sharing our rubber tip.

Rita Rudner

I'm feeling claustrophobic. It must be you.

43. Decorated with Honors

Some people just have the knack. They can buy an old chair at a garage sale for peanuts, do it up (I'd be more specific if I could, but I'm not sure what they do), and it looks like it cost a fortune. I, on the other hand, can find a chair that costs a fotune, and people will ask me, "Did you get that at a garage sale?"

I really tried with my first apartment. Before then furniture was not something that I ever gave much thought to, but there I was—eighteen and living alone in New York with nothing to sit on. I did my best with my limited budget and my even more limited imagination to create an environment that was unique and special. Imagine how proud I was when I invited my first New York friend over for coffee and she looked around and said, "This is great; did you rent it furnished?"

"Yes," I said, not wanting to get into it.

"Well, this will be a great apartment when you get rid of this stuff and buy your own."

"Yes," I repeated, hoping she would leave because not only did I not know how to decorate an apartment, I wasn't real sure how to make coffee.

What had happened was, because I had just been on the road with a show for a year and been living in hotel rooms, I had accidentally decorated my apartment in what can only be described as "Early Howard Johnson's." I tried to make the place a little more homey by buying some plants, but I later found out I should have bought some that were real.

The one thing I had not purchased for my "pied à hotel room" was a rug. I was determined to pick one that was an expression of myself, not of Mr. Johnson. I was so determined to express myself that I brought along my friend to tell me what I liked. She took me to one of those "going out of business stores" so I could get one cheap.

"Shouldn't we go to a department store?" I asked. "What if something goes wrong and I have to return it and the store has gone out of business?"

"You'll pay twice as much in a department store," she said. "These stores never go out of business. Look how old their 'Going out of Business' sign is. It's been there for twenty years."

While we perused the store, strange men held up large matted wads of wool in front of us and yelled, "This is beautiful. This is for you."

My friend and I decided I liked a simple blue-and-white-patterned Chinese carpet. She then had to leave, but I was confident that she knew what I liked and all I had to do was get out my checkbook and pay for it. I got out my checkbook, looked up, and another strange man was holding up another rug in front of me and saying, "This is beautiful. This is for you."

My friend hadn't seen this rug. Maybe it was more beautiful than the rug we had decided on. It was twice as expensive, so it must be more beautiful. I held my breath and decided to trust my newfound taste. I wrote out a check for five hundred dollars and asked when they could deliver it.

"Deliver it? We don't deliver . . . well, maybe for fifty dollars extra."

It was either that or take a ten-foot-by-twelve-foot rug home on a bus.

"When can you deliver it?" I asked.

"Two weeks."

"Two weeks?"

"For eighty dollars extra, maybe one week."

The department store savings were disappearing into the sunset.

A week later I sat in my apartment praying that I hadn't made a terrible mistake. The buzzer rang. It was the doorman.

"There are two strange men coming up carrying a very loud carpet."

It was not sounding good. I opened the door. They said, "Here is your carpet, lady," and started to leave.

I said, "Aren't you going to unroll it?"

They said, "For an extra fifty dollars."

I paid them for the fourth time and sat in the room

An Outroduction

you've enjoyed reading this book as much as I've
d writing it. There are two things you can do in
ood where you can maintain creative control: you
er write a book or have a baby. They both take nine
and they both keep you up all night. The big dif-
s books don't borrow money and marry people you
ve of . . . at least that's what my publisher told me.

with my brand-new rug. It definitely did not belong in a
Howard Johnson's. It belonged in a Chinese whorehouse. I
tried to live with it for a few days, but it was so loud, it
burned my feet. I had made a terrible mistake. I called the
store. It had gone out of business. I called two handymen
and paid them fifty dollars to take it out of my apartment
and burn it. I went to a department store and bought the
rug I originally wanted at a lower price with free delivery.

I've come up in the world since then. I've traveled, and
I think I've developed a sense of style. I just decorated a
whole house, and I'm proud to say no one has said it reminds
them of a Howard Johnson's. It reminds them of a Hyatt.

44. Title Fight

When I finished this book I was elated. I then realized I hadn't finished this book. I said good-bye to elation and tried to think of a title. What follows is a list of runners-up.

Fake Pearls of Wisdom

Has Anyone Seen My Sunglasses?

Rita Rudner and 'Rithmetic

The Pith Myth

The Luck Stops Here

If It's on Fire, Don't Lay Down on It

If Life Is a Cabaret, I'm Sitting Behind Someone with Very Big Hair

Nothing Rhymes with Rudner

How to Wallpaper Your Car

A Funny Thing Happened to

Guilty of Innocence

Speak Softly and Wear a Bi

There's Only One Thing I'r
What It Is

Do I Have Lipstick on My

Wake Up and Smell the

The Best Things in Life

I Think These Things So

Nearsighted Insights

I hope
enjoyed
Hollyw
can eith
months,
ference
disappro